Khoda Hafez...Goodbye Iran

*Cover Photo: Nora listening to the BBC news on our battery radio
during the Tehran blackouts.*

Khoda Hafez…Goodbye Iran

June 1978 to January 1979

John Doolittle

Write My Wrongs Co, United States
www.writemywrongsediting.com

Copyright © 2022 John Doolittle

Dedicated to Nora, my wife, mother of my children, and best friend for fifty-five years (and still going strong). Without her help, input, and support, this adventure and book would have never happened.

Contents

PREFACE

This is a story about Tehran, Iran, in 1978 and what happened while we lived there.

As Shah Mohammad Reza Pahlavi's control over his empire started to erode, there were demonstrations throughout the country. I have not covered those incidents in detail other than the theater fire in the city of Abadan, which is located in southern Iran. I've used many quotes from newspapers to give readers a sense of what the media thought was important regarding Iran. In a few cases, I found misspellings of Iranian names and words. If the error was one letter, I changed it. If the correction resulted in a new spelling of the word, I put the corrected spelling in [brackets] behind the word.

To relate the news stories to what was actually happening, as reflected in my notes, I have moved many stories back one day or more and eliminated the word "yesterday" from the news reports and replaced it with ellipses ("…"). In some cases, I only quoted parts of the stories that pertained to Tehran and our immediate surroundings. In these instances, you will see ". …" for the part eliminated. I did correct any obvious spelling errors, but other than that, the quotes are accurate. I have my own notes, notes from Nora (all her notes and letters are in *italics*), and many articles from the *Kayhan International* newspaper. It is also interspersed with memos from American Bell International Incorporated (ABII) (which were given to me as an employee) and other news sources (e.g., the *San Francisco Chronicle*, Santa Rosa *Press Democrat*). All the sources I used have been documented in the endnotes, and I have been liberal in direct quotations. Nora's letters to her parents and my parents are prefaced by *Dear Mom and Dad*. It really doesn't make much difference which set of parents got the letter for the purposes of this book. You will also be able to see some of what the media covered and said during this time. In many cases, it's interesting to see the difference in perspectives in what we saw and experienced versus what was reported.

In most of the quoted articles, a follower of Islam was referred to as a "Moslem." In today's vernacular; however, the proper word is "Muslim." For any article I quoted, I left the word as written, while in my writings I used Muslim. Consider Moslem to be Muslim.

ABII's preparation and ongoing support for this Tehran assignment was excellent. My entire family visited the Hadley Road facility in New Jersey for training and an introduction to Farsi, the language spoken in Iran. We received numerous briefings on how life would be different and how to deal with these differences. The New Jersey staff was most professional, and that same professionalism carried over while we were in Tehran. ABII made sure we were kept abreast of all the latest developments in Tehran, as can be seen by the numerous security and notice alerts quoted. Every detail regarding safety was addressed. We couldn't have been more pleased with the support.

This is a "blink in time" from when we lived in Iran from June 12, 1978, to January 16, 1979. Hopefully, you, the reader, will be able to get a sense of the atmosphere around us as Iranians went through significant changes in how they lived and how they were governed. It's a time few experienced or remember.

When President Carter was elected in 1976, his policies stressed more support for Iranian human rights than support for the monarchy. But I believe too much was done too quickly. The end result is what this book is about. It reminds us that a democracy cannot be imposed from the top down but must rise from the bottom up; the people must want it.

One thought to keep in mind when evaluating the actions and thoughts of Iranians—they have a different mindset than Westerners. The mindset is not wrong, just different. What makes sense to us may not make sense to them, and what does not make sense to us may make perfect sense to them.

His Royal Majesty Mohammad Reza Pahlavi was born October 26, 1919, and ruled Iran from 1941 to February 1979. Ayatollah Sayyid Ruhollah Musavi Khomeini was born May 17, 1900, and was instrumental in supporting a revolution against the monarchy from Paris until he arrived in Iran on February 1, 1979. In March of 1979, the monarchy was officially replaced with an Islamic republic. My intention is to not cover the historical detail leading up to the formation of the republic but to give a perspective of what it was like to live in Iran as the transition from a monarchy to an Islamic republic took place. To help put this story in focus, it takes place during the events that led up to the end of the Shah's rule and ends a little less than ten months before the U.S. embassy takeover on November 4, 1979 (i.e., the Iran hostage crisis). The political figures are not my focus. Instead, I want to give readers a feeling of what it was like to live in Tehran during this time, interacting with ordinary Iranians and employees of ABII. As you read, keep in mind it is possible to dislike the political position of a government or a dissident and still love the people of another country.

This is Iran.

PROLOGUE

Monday, May 29, 1978

"Dear Mr. Doolittle:

On behalf of American Bell International Incorporated (ABII), I am pleased to offer you a position as senior engineer (AB-7) in our Network Project Management Organization effective June 4, 1978, reporting to Mr. L.A. Sozzi. The work of this organization is conducted in Tehran, Iran, where staff members work a forty-hour, five-day week. You will be placed on indefinite leave of absence from Pacific Telephone and Telegraph Company for the duration of this assignment. Your Bell System Net Credited Service date of April 12, 1971, is continued. Pacific Telephone and Telegraph Company has agreed to accept you upon your return from ABII at a position of like status to that held by you prior to joining ABII. The expected length of your assignment is two to three years. Upon completion of twenty months on this assignment, you and your supervision will decide when you should return to your home company. Your assignment may be lengthened or shortened as necessitated by the needs of the business; however, prior to your return to your home company, 120-days' notice will be required to both ABII and Pacific Telephone and Telegraph Company."

The rest of the letter contained details regarding the job: salary, incentives, medical requirements, security clearances, family requirements, etc. It closed with, "Please indicate, by your signature, that you have read and understand the contents of this letter. Retain the original of the letter for your files and return a signed copy in the envelope provided."

I signed it that night.

***

Monday, June 12, 1978

I opened my eyes. Iran Air's 747 had started its decent into Mehrabad International Airport, Tehran, Iran. It had been an eighteen-hour flight from San Francisco via London. There was a haze over the entire area, making the mountains, countryside, and city all the same brown color, except for the little snow on the tops of the peaks behind the city. Most people think Tehran is in the middle of the desert, when in reality, it's four thousand feet above sea level, and it even snows in the city during the wintertime.

As the plane started its descent, I thought back to what I was doing, taking my wife and two children for a three-year assignment in Iran. I left California, a comfortable middle-management job, a dog, a nice home, and lots of friends to come halfway around the world to a new job. I thought it was the "right time" in my life for a little adventure, and with a big company backing me, what could be safer? While my friends and family expressed concern for leaving the comfort and safety of the United States and going to a "third world" country, I reasoned Iran was stable and moving toward a progressing lifestyle for its people.

I graduated from Occidental College in Southern California with a major in economics. After a four-year tour in the U.S. Air Force serving as a captain, I joined the Pacific Bell Telephone and Telegraph Company (Pac Bell) as a manager. I continued my education, receiving an MBA in finance from Cal Berkeley, and also stayed with the air force as a reserve officer. My telephone career had progressed nicely, but then an opportunity came up—a senior engineering job in Tehran, Iran. I had taken a job with ABII, who had a contract with the Imperial Government of Iran to assist in building Iran's telecommunications network from eight hundred thousand lines to over five million in ten years, an ambitious and challenging objective. Iran's population at the time was 36 million people; Tehran was 4.8 million. As senior engineer, my job involved setting up program controls and monitoring progress on all the ABII projects. My new ABII boss didn't care if I wasn't actually an engineer but selected me based on my work in the military. I was to work with the Shah's military to establish a "status room" to report the progress of converting the Iranian telephone system into a first-class telephone company to serve a high percentage of Iran's population.

So there I was, about to land in a foreign country with my entire family, knowing only a few phrases of an unfamiliar language, ready for a job I knew little about. Nora rested against my shoulder, sleeping. We had been married for ten years. I loved her more than anything in the world. The only other two people who came close were our children: John, who was eight, and Tori, who was four. Nora and I met at college, where we dated on and off for four years before deciding there was no one else for either of us. We had been married in a beautiful military ceremony at the San Gabriel Mission right after my graduation from Air Force Officer Training School. Prior to accepting the assignment, we spent several months discussing how our family would fit in Iran. Nora was a slender blonde, and both children were definitely American in appearance. Women with blonde hair in Iran were both unusual and conspicuous, inviting curious stares. But despite a few misgivings, Nora shared my sense of adventure and looked forward to our new life.

As the 747 dropped in altitude, I could see the massive construction going on throughout Tehran. Tall cranes were everywhere, especially along the main highway leading to the airport. In the distance, one could just make out the Shahyad Monument, or the Azadi Tower, which had been built by the Shah in 1971 to commemorate the 2,500th year of the foundation of the Imperial State of Iran. I woke Nora up, giving her a little kiss on the head. Both kids were sitting across the aisle and listening to music through their headsets. The stewardess walked through the cabin one more time to make sure everyone had their seatbelts on, and the 747 started its final descent into Mehrabad Airport. John and Tori jammed their faces against the window to look at the strange new country. I whispered to Nora, "Let the adventure begin."

Processing through customs didn't take much time. I had been told it was leaving the country that could be a problem. Once we were done getting our passports stamped and collecting our luggage, it was off to our new home. I had already made arrangements through work for a place to live. It was in the north part of the city to take advantage of the cool air during the summer. Tehran was built on a gentle slope, so the south section, below the bazaar, was much hotter in the summer than the northern area, where the Shah's palace was located. The most northern part of town was in the foothills of the Alborz Mountains. Up on the slopes of the mountains, the Shah had built a state-of-the-art ski resort, Dizin.

My new boss, Leo Sozzi, met us at the airport. After introductions, he got us settled into a large cab. As we moved through town, I pointed out new things to the children. There was a hot beet seller on the corner who had his own cooker to heat the beets. A Coke truck passed the cab as we drove by the gold and brass stores that lined the street. Saltanatabad Boulevard, which was the main artery of northern Tehran, was four lanes wide in each direction with trees lining the street itself. The green of the foliage and the grass were a deep contrast to the bland marble buildings and clay brick storefronts.

Before going to our new home, Leo took us to a grocery store. He helped us purchase what he thought we would need in the "short term."Once I paid for the groceries, Leo told me it was customary to tip the boys who helped us take the bags to the car. I reached in my wallet and pulled out what I thought was a five-dollar tip in rials and handed the bills to the boys. Their eyes opened wide as they ripped off their aprons and ran down the street yelling in joy. I asked Leo what happened. He told me I had just tipped the boys fifty dollars' worth of rials, which was almost more than the groceries had cost. Lesson learned.

As we continued to our new lodging, we passed a school, and the children were at recess. It looked just like home, everyone running around with two or three teachers monitoring their activities. The cab continued up the street. The whole family could feel the air getting cooler as we got closer to the mountains. After several turns, the cab finally went left onto a residential street. It was quiet; no one was on the road. There were no front yards, only walled-in marble patios. On each side of the road was an open ditch about a foot wide and there were a few dogs playing in water at the bottom of the trough. I asked the driver what those ditches were. He told us they were "jube ditches" or toilets. We all knew then Tehran was not like any neighborhood in the United States.

THE ONSET

Thursday, June 15, 1978

We arrived safe and sound, and we're extremely pleased with everything. Our new home is in the northeast section of Tehran, near work, and in the same general area as the Shah's palace. We live in a duplex made of marble that's twice as big as our house in Pleasant Hill. It has four and a half bedrooms, two baths, a living room, and a swimming pool we share with another ABII family living below us (a family of two adults, three children, two longhaired dachshunds, and two *koocheh*/street cats).Their kids and ours became friends quickly. The street we live on is small and lined with trees that were planted about every three feet.

The Saltanatabad-Darrus area, where we live, looks exactly like Pasadena, California, except the mountains still have snow (*barf* in Farsi). The Iranians are very friendly and enjoy helping us learn Farsi, the native language in Iran. My boss, Leo, is young and very nice. He, his wife, and his two children have taken us in tow these past few days. Today is Thursday, our first "Saturday," since the work week is Saturday to Wednesday. We walked around and did a little shopping. The food is good, but about 25 to 50 percent more expensive. Some American products are 600 percent more. While we were out, I learned something else. Iranian drivers drive like pilots going in for a strike—fast and accurate.

***

Saturday, June 17, 1978

Today was my first day of work. Workdays are Saturday through Wednesday, six forty five in the morning to three fifteen in the afternoon. Steve Parker, who lives below us, works in the same building, so we went to work together. On Thursday (our Saturday), the entire Program Control group (which I am a part of) moved to a new location. I asked Steve if he knew where my group would be working. He said probably the seventh floor. When we arrived, the elevator was still being installed, so we walked up the fire escape. The building is brand new and still under construction from the ninth floor up. Upon reaching the seventh floor, I noticed construction material, tables, and desks littering the hall. There was a coating of construction dust over everything. I thought Steve had given me the wrong floor, so I was getting ready to walk down to the sixth floor to see if it looked any better when I decided to check out the seventh floor entirely before going elsewhere. I walked into rooms, stepping over piles of dirt and concrete. I saw more Americans and asked them where Leo Sozzi's office was. They said down the hall on the left. So down the hall I walked, looking for door numbers or name plates. I noticed little scraps of paper with Farsi numbers and English names. At the end of the hall, I found Leo's office with a broken desk, no electricity, no chair, no telephone, and everything covered in dust. There I waited for Leo.

At seven thirty he walked in and said hello. He then showed me my office, which was a big room across the hall with nothing in it. In walked George Tears, another of Leo's subordinates, and we made introductions. George and I grabbed some desks from other offices—the early bird gets the worm—and started housekeeping.

Today was a day of learning. The nearest telephone for the seventh floor was on the third floor, and the nearest working drinking fountain and bathroom were also on the third floor. The elevator finally started working at three thirty, fifteen minutes after closing time. The electricity was off all day with no forecast of when it would come on. The division level manager's office didn't have any glass in the windows (I had glass in both windows, but only one window could be opened at a time). When I went home, the Iranian drivers switched the minibus numbers, so the 250 people pouring out of the building at three fifteen either got on the wrong bus or were left trying to figure out if the bus they missed was the right or wrong one. I gave up and waited for Steve to go home at four, since he had his own car. As long as everyone here kept a sense of humor, items and incidents as described above become comical. My job would be dealing with the military, which I enjoyed already.

Nora and the kids adapted quickly. My son, John, and I went to church on Friday, which was our Sunday.

Dear Mom and Dad,

Well, we made it with the entire luggage, and everyone is still healthy. Our house is really nice, and the best thing is the kids' ages who live under us—eight, six, and three. They get along with John and Tori very well. The kids seem to know over here that they need to be nice to one another, so they have friends. We have four and a half bedrooms, two baths, washer-dryer, and floor-to-ceiling drapes in every room. We have a nice yard with green lawn and roses, and a pool we share with just the Parkers. They are another ABII family. It is a perfect setup, and they ski too. They invited us down for chicken Thursday night.

Claire and I walked up to the koocheek *(small) store. I must say, I didn't feel like eating the vegetables, but we* Rokal *(bleach) them, and no one got sick. I had heard so many bad things about Tehran that I am pleasantly surprised. It doesn't smell; the jubes (sewage ditches by the road) water the trees in our area, which line the street about two to three feet apart. Pahlavi Boulevard is the longest tree-lined street in the world. The trees near us are about twenty feet high, and the house is made of marble with a marble driveway. The building materials amaze me. Our fence and all the floors in the apartment are marble—wood is a luxury, and grass, trees, and pools are more precious than electricity to the Iranians. In a water shortage, electricity is cut first. Claire has a maid, so I will get one. Iranians feel that children should not have duties or jobs. Children aren't responsible for anything.*

John's boss, Leo Sozzi, along with his family, met us at the airport. Our home is nicer than theirs, according to Leo. I'll never know how we

3

were so lucky. Judy, Leo's wife, took John and me grocery shopping on Tuesday and then had us over for dinner that night. Prices are high, but if you buy Iranian, it is cheaper. Tuna is two dollars per can, but funny, there is no difference between regular and white tuna. Paper napkins are two dollars for one hundred, which surprised me. We spent one hundred dollars, and now I have to go to the store again four days later. I found good ham and hamburger, and Claire's Iranian chicken is good. Tonight, we will have lamb chops. I even found "Spray and Wash" for $3.50 and a small bleach for $4.38. That is a little expensive, but there are things I feel we need. John wants "regular" mayonnaise, and that costs six dollars a jar. Last week, we had Iranian spaghetti, and it wasn't too bad. Tori is the one I worry about with food. She isn't eating much. I guess I will have to buy some peanut butter.

Our gardener comes every day to water, plant, and clip; he only cost sixty dollars a month. Labor is so cheap. We have a beautiful two-story mosaic of an Iranian horseman on the wall, which extends two stories from the Parkers' up through our place. We are the only ones who can enjoy this. Banks in Pleasant Hill would never loan money for it to be built. It is funny how my parameters have changed from the City of Pleasant Hill to the County of Contra Costa to the State of California; now, we refer to the United States as "the States". Things appear to move very slowly around here. I have a feeling my biggest frustration will be there are too many Americans after the same things I'm after.

I was late for orientation because the taxi services were busy. I can't enroll the kids in summer school, and Tori has to go on a waiting list for swimming lessons. Driving around in a taxi is an adventure. The other day, we came upon a Datsun 260Z abandoned in the middle of an intersection and a car upside down in a ditch. Going the wrong way on a one-way street is a serious traffic violation; however, if the taxi backs up on the same street, it is all right. It really isn't as bad as all the stories. Our friends with the two girls from Hadley Row (NJ) just called, and they live within walking distance from us. Another girl from Hadley Row called too. I really like our neighbor, Claire. She is positive about everything.

John just came home from his first day of work. The building isn't finished yet. They had to walk up the fire escape because the elevator isn't working yet. There are no telephones, electricity, or glass in the windows. There is no place to eat lunch, and the buses were all fouled *up, so no one knew how to get home. My part of this assignment may be easier than his. No problems at home except we have to push the button on the hot water heater about once a day for hot water.*

"Soldiers with fixed bayonets stood by at key points in this holy city [Qom]…but a stay-at-home strike by thousands of conservative Moslems remained peaceful and seemed to signal at least a temporary end to Iran's six-month-long cycle of anti-government violence.

Tehran, Iran's capital 75 miles north of Qom, also was calm, with businesses open as usual. Tehran's university campuses have been a focal point for unrest in the past, but students are on summer vacation.

The Shiite leadership has been concerned about the weakening of traditional family patterns, which they blame on such Western influences as sex movies and increasing freedom for women. They say the modernization program of Shah Mohammad Reza Pahlavi's government is responsible.

Moslem traditionalists also demand implementation of a never-used clause in Iran's 1906 constitution that would give them a final say over new legislation. Secular political groups opposed to authoritarian aspects of the shah's rule have joined in the protests."[1]

***

Sunday, June 18, 1978

As I walked up the fire escape at work, I heard yelling from up above. Our division manager, whose office had no glass in the windows, had left stacks of paper on his desk. But wind came up overnight, and the papers he left were all over his office, down the hall, and in the stairwell. He was not happy and was scrambling, dressed in his suit, after papers as they continued to blow away from him. He yelled the whole time. It was not considered a serious issue by those of us watching and trying to help, but it did lend a little humor to the morning. As I walked into my office, George had tea ready. It was going to be a good day.

***

Tuesday, June 20, 1978

Today is our sixteenth day with ABII and our eighth day in Iran. After being here for a week, I have found that I'm assigned to probably one of the "hottest" areas in the Seek Switch Program (the name of the entire project): Program Control. It's a totally unstructured environment with parameters constantly changing at the discretion of the government.

Tonight, it hailed and rained for about fifteen minutes, just enough to clear the air. Last night, at the officer's club (for the military assigned in Tehran), I found out I qualify for a membership since I'm in the Air Force Reserve, which means we can eat American meals every so often.

***

Thursday, June 22, 1978

Today, the entire family visited the Shahyad Monument. Underground was a museum, which gave us all the history of the amazing country of Iran.

There are certain things here that are very different from the United States. They aren't wrong, just different. Driving is one of these. I do as little driving as possible, mostly whenever visiting outside the city. Within the city, though, I take a cab. It is against the law to drive the wrong way on a one-way street, but it's legal to back up on one-way streets as fast as one would drive forward. When making a left-hand turn, to make it a challenge, the cab gets in the right-hand lane and then turns left. It is a feat accompanied by yelling and horn honking, a macho experience. Some drivers in the city could get speeding tickets from policemen who watched the car go by and wrote the license number down. But there's no apprehension or warning that the ticket has been given. ABII will get the violation, see who had checked out the car, and present them with the ticket.

Tonight, we had dinner with a new ABII couple at the German Hotel. It was an excellent outdoor meal by the pool and goldfish, followed by three bottles of wine and dancing. It only cost 4,200 rials (thirty-two U.S. dollars) per couple. The band played everything from the Blue Danube to Russian and Iranian folk dances to American rock. It was an outstanding evening.

ABII Notice

"The German Hotel is a favorite night spot for many ABIIers. The food is good, and the atmosphere is great. There's a garden, a pool with goldfish and fountains, and there's dancing under the stars. A full meal including cheese, bread and butter, soup, salad, entrée, ice cream or compote, and tea or coffee runs about 500–700 rials. Entrées include the usual continental selections and some German specialties like sauerbraten and red cabbage. Of course, there are drinks. For groups, setups and bottles of scotch or bourbon may be ordered for your table. The band is a big plus. They are very good, and they play something for everyone."[2]

***

Friday, June 23, 1978

We visited the Madhoks and walked to one of Tehran's larger parks. Raj Madhok was my old boss from Pacific Bell who came to Tehran earlier with his family. It was a relatively clear day with balmy weather. We had a lamb kabob for lunch. They actually ran out of lamb just as we ordered, but the waiter said not to worry. A few minutes later, we saw a lamb being led to a spot behind the restaurant. The lamb started to cry out but was cut short by the sound of an axe. So we had fresh kabob. Next week, it will be our turn to entertain. We will be cooking (probably hamburgers) for the Madhoks and the Parkers.

Son John has already found a new play area. There's a construction site near us, where workers shovel dirt on a screen to get the rocks out, and John retrieves the rocks to use with his Star Wars figures. There is also a three-inch lip in the garage under our home. Using his yellow skateboard, John got his first "air" off the lip!

Just as an aside regarding work items: the manholes over here are square—so it's easier for people to fall in—and the telephone poles are cement and owned by the power company. The telephone company has attached its wires to the side of the cement poles. Drop lines are then attached to the houses from the main line, and they are truly "drop" lines because they're just hanging from the pole to the house. The Shah has done a great job building parks and planting trees. Most of northern Tehran is covered with green growth.

Dear Mom and Dad,

Well, the mail is difficult around here. First off, one has to know enough Farsi to get to a post office and understand the money exchange enough to buy stamps. Second, you just hope the mail goes out. We were walking along Pahlavi Boulevard today, and there was a mailbox wide open with all the letters inside, all the mail exposed to anyone who passed by. The ABII building I could use for mail isn't the same one John works in; it is downtown, and the taxi drivers don't like going there. John doesn't get much mail at his office either because it is on the seventh floor with no electricity, elevators, or phones. One has to go up the outside fire escape to reach him. It is a new building and isn't completed yet. It is amazing how they build. Everything is with bricks and steel. There are no wood beams. The floors are bricks and mortar.

Everything is running smoothly, except the pool pump is broken, and chlorine is fifteen dollars for a small bottle, but the kids are still swimming and healthy. I noticed Iranians sleep during the day from noon to four. The women just wrap up in their chadors and go to sleep on the grass in the parks. The Iranians seem to like blonde children and women, so I feel "in." Our taxi driver gave me a plum today, and I ate it without washing it...and I'm still healthy.

***

Monday, June 26, 1978

We have been in our Iran home two weeks as of today. Already, it is difficult to remember Pleasant Hill and Pacific Bell. Seems like we've been here a year, but I'm not sure if that is good or bad. We're quickly making friends and entering the Iranian social life. This Thursday, we're hosting a barbeque for our neighbors and the Madhoks. Last night, Steve Parker and I fixed the filter on our pool. Tonight, we repaired our telephone because we couldn't break dial tone on our party line. Steve's background was installation and repair, so he felt the two of us could fix it. He attached the phone to the terminal box and, by process of elimination, discovered the problem was in the drop line from the pole to the house. Since it was the responsibility of the subscriber to maintain the drop line, we trotted off to the hardware store for some wire. We brought the wire, strung it, hooked it up, and presto, a working telephone.

Program Control, where I work, has been recognized as the key part to the whole ABII program. Consequently, we are very busy. Through our "Monitoring and Control Room" (hereafter called the Status Room), we give updates to the general who is responsible for funding the program and reporting progress to the Shah. The purpose of the room is to display the status of major projects in the Seek Switch Expansion Program that provide telephone service to Tehran and other areas of Iran. Emphasis is placed on projects encountering delays. Telecommunication Company of Iran (TCI) and ABII will constantly be improving, updating, and enlarging upon the information displayed in here. I spent most of this morning talking to fellow employees about switching, transmission, facilities, and microwave systems. I learned more about the telephone business in this past week than I did all of last year.

It's amazing what an assignment like this does for one's insight. Things we always take for granted, such as Miracle Whip, peanut butter, and Oreo cookies, suddenly become luxury items. Rush hour driving really isn't too bad, but Iran traffic laws allow backing up on one-way streets. Yesterday, my cab backed up at full speed for three blocks because he missed the turn. On the other side of the coin, the simple life is fun. I haven't brought work home once because you can't. All work must stay at the office. My boss and I leave at the same time to catch the minibus home. I get home at three thirty, which gives me time to do a lot of things with Nora and the kids. Iranians take things much slower here. If you can't get it done today, there's always tomorrow, next week, or even next month. The kids have adjusted easily, and Nora is already looking forward to the school year starting (wonder why). Television stations are so much easier; there is only one channel from four in the afternoon to eleven in the evening. No fuss, no bother.

***

Wednesday, June 28, 1978

Today, George and I were asked not to pour the old tea out of our seventh-story window since it was leaving a stain on the outside marble. Later on in the day, I walked around the building and looked up at our window. Yep, I could see a stain. Hopefully, the winter rain will remove it.

We attended an ABII softball game followed by pizza and beer at an Iranian restaurant. Mike Terry and Terry Scott were playing. After dinner, we adjourned to our house.

Dear Mom and Dad,

It has been two weeks now, and I'm not ready to pack my bags and leave. I had one bad Iranian day, which I'll tell you about. Sunday, John went to work as usual. I was going to take son John down to look at horseback riding lessons, but the phone didn't work. Claire took her kids to a friend's house for the day, so her cab was free to drop the three of us off at the Stevensons'. Unfortunately, they weren't home, so we started walking home.

There isn't any entertainment at home. The filter on the pool is broken. There is so much chlorine in the water that Tori's arms are chapped, and John's feet have cracked and are bleeding in places. It is hot, and they both complained as we walked all the way home. I can cope without a car and without a phone, but not without both. I purchased some cortisone cream for John's feet for 150 rials ($2.20), and I bought loads of plants today, so our house is looking like home. I spent 2,600 rials and got two palms, one fern, four geraniums, one small fern, one spider plant, two pothos, a coleus, and a basket. I gave the coleus to Claire's maid. She washed my steps for me and gave us flowers the first two weeks we were here. Our pool pump looks like a coffee pot with vacuum cleaner hoses on it, but it works! I think my biggest adjustments here are how to handle a servant relationship on friendly and nice terms, how to tip, and how to deal with a taxi driver who has overstepped his bounds. Everyone is so nice to me; it must be the blonde hair. Please try to send us as many coat hangers as you can cheaply. I think anything under two pounds is reasonable.

***

Thursday, June 29, 1978

John and Tori figured out that if they put a bowl of milk on the ledge next to the pool, all the local cats will come and drink. A lot of stray cats—great! I also had to put a stop to six-foot jumps off the wall's ledge near the pool, over the surrounding fence and into the pool. We did not want unnecessary visits to the local hospital.

The Madhoks, Mike Terry, and Terry Scott came over for dinner and a swim. Nora and I fed sixteen people using only our "hospitality kit" (one glass, seven plates, and two platters), which was probably a first. Claire made potato salad, and Nora made two cakes in frying pans.

***

Friday, June 30, 1978

Today, we joined the Parkers and a bachelor friend for a swim day. Dinner was Colonel Sanders's barbecued chicken for all of us. We feel so fortunate to live above the Parkers. The job continues to be very interesting. I found out Wednesday that I may be working for a new district-level manager this week. The job is being redefined, and I may work for a fellow who currently has the construction budget. The magnitude of this job and the entire ABII project is almost overwhelming when one considers we are not only bringing lines to five million people in Tehran but also setting up a satellite program.

We were scheduled to call Nora's parents tonight, but one of the transmission lines was down, so we rescheduled it for July 4. Raj Madhok is checking out the possibility of our two families securing an ABII minibus and driving to the Caspian Sea. We are hoping to do this the first week of August. The kids are finally asleep tonight. I'm reading *Armageddon* by L. Uris. It's excellent. Nora went on a "plant tour" this week with other ABII women, and our home now has lots of plants.

Dear Mom and Dad,

Our sink got clogged, and John certainly missed his tools but then found that all he had to do was unscrew the pipes by hand. Claire's

11

maid is getting me a maid, who is coming tomorrow for the interview, and I have no idea what I'm supposed to do or ask. I do hope she will know some English. I think she costs ten dollars a day, and I will use her three days.

My plants are still growing. I sprayed them with my bleach bottle. The bugs in the furniture have grown accustomed to me so no more bug bites. John's feet are better and so are Tori's arms. My John still has no bathroom or telephone on his floor, and the elevator does not work (he is on the seventh floor).We are anxiously awaiting our baggage from home. I used most of my plates by placing them under the plants. Tori had a taco at the pizza place, and it fell apart on her first bite; it looked like Fritos. She cried and thought it was her fault. We are having fun.

***

Sunday, July 2, 1978

Dear Mom and Dad,

Well, I now have a baji, or a maid, three times a week, so I am free to come and go as I please. This is her first day, and she seems like a good worker. Everything is going fine, and I think I will find plenty to do to keep me busy around here. The biggest thing is keeping the kids occupied this summer. The Parkers and their kids are going back to the States for six weeks. What will I do without them? I think little John is getting bored. Well, now the men are hanging the drapes, so it is really starting to look like home.

I bought all sorts of plants last week so it doesn't look so sterile and have looked at furniture. The company pays seven hundred dollars toward new replacements, which really isn't very much, but I just found out they owe us a rug. Someone "walked off" with it before we moved in. It has really been hot, but so far, our air conditioner is working. Poor John is still on the seventh floor with no air conditioning or an elevator.

Your comments in your last letter about the California education make me glad we are here for the kid's education. We just went up to the store to look for wine, a most interesting walk passing the Mercedes, $250K homes, the ladies and their chadors, the sheep herders, and traffic. We went to three koocheek stores and finally back to Super Parmis, our America-has-everything store. The maid did the washing, *floors, and ironing, and it does look better. I had saved my paints for when the kids were bored…today was a good time to use them. John just got back from Super Parmis, and it was closed. He just missed it. Tomorrow is an Iranian holiday, and John doesn't go to work. We are going to see a friend of his from work who has a little girl in son John's class.*

***

Monday, July 3, 1978

We went to Gordon Griffes' home (my new boss starting July 15) to swim and have dinner. They have two girls, Lynn and Hilary, ages seven and thirteen.

Dear Mom and Dad,

Just got back from the Griffeses. They have really collected some beautiful things. Joan is going to take me junk shopping Saturday, assuming my maid works out, and I can leave the kids. She collects bags and makes pillows out of them. They are very unique and just beautiful.

Little John had diarrhea today and says it hurts to walk. He seems to be the only one with that problem. He got to stay up late to take a shower, so Tori immediately said, "No fair; my bottom hurts too." Kids!

Did this letter take much longer than my Air Grams? I don't think the mail is as big a deal as it was made out to be. We have been trying to collect the ingredients for chocolate chip cookies for two weeks, and now all I need is baking soda. The Parkers are having a party Friday, so I will make them for that. I think there is a big Fourth of July party next weekend, where we get hamburgers and real buns!

We haven't heard too much about student demonstrations here. I know some people who are going to California for Christmas; Terry Scott is going home and will return after Christmas. His wife, Linda, left and is not coming back. I am glad we brought mostly clothing because that is the most expensive thing to get here. I brought those little green 3M scrub things, and they are three for forty-five cents here, so that wasn't necessary. They have Woolite, Spray & Wash, bleach, and Top Job and aren't priced unreasonably. Cokes are very cheap once you buy the bottles, and vodka is cheap. So are cucumbers and yogurt, all very healthy things. I made the mistake of sleeping until nine this morning, and then took a nap this afternoon, so, although it is late, I'm not tired. John is asleep, as he has to work tomorrow.

Claire and I will shop for brooms for our maids tomorrow. Ours wants a work dress also. We will see what happens. I didn't tell John that was part of the deal. It is very late now, so I will write more tomorrow. We are all fine and like it here. I feel sorry for John working in this heat on the seventh floor with no elevator or air conditioning, but I guess if the kids and I stay happy, he is happy too. He gets home at three thirty! He gets a chance to sit around the pool, play with the filter along with Steve, mow the lawn with a push mower—which has only one-wheel which turns—cook dinner sometimes, and take walks when it is cooler. He never brings any work home, and his job doesn't entail organizing Iranians, which can be a big frustration. Back in the States, bosses get upset when a report isn't in on time. Over here, the secretary doesn't have a typewriter that works, she gets stuck in the elevator, she may have the "runs" and is sick, has no transportation, or the person who is supposed to write the report never even did it. As long as one keeps a sense of humor about it, work is funny. John and Steve fixed the phone. They actually purchased wire from the hardware store, ran it from the pole to the apartment, and connected it. Without that, we would still be without a phone.

ABII Notice

"July 3 is the Moslem holiday of Eid-e-Mabas. ABII will be closed to observe it.

It is a joyous holiday when Moslems celebrate the day that their leader, Mohammad, was called by God to serve as his prophet. ...The miracle of Mohammad's enlightenment is the Koran, the Holy Book of Islam. Through divine intervention and suggestion, he was able to write this book which contains wisdom, insight, and prophecy. ...

Most Moslems mark this holiday with prayer and good cheer. Family visits and relaxation are enjoyed. Green flags and lights may be seen decorating the mosques. A Sal'aam ceremony is held at the palace of His Imperial Majesty, the Shahanshah."[3]

***

Tuesday, July 4, 1978

We worked today. To help celebrate the Fourth of July, I put our flag up in the backyard.

Dear Mom and Dad,
I wish we could find some maple syrup for pancakes. That is the only thing we haven't found a substitute for. You wouldn't believe this, but I have read two books on biblical prophecies. If things keep going the way they are and a powerful ruler emerges out of Rome, I may become a Jehovah's Witness. The book is called The Last Great Planet Earth *by Hal Lindsey.*
John got his first paycheck, and I don't understand any of it, where the money is or our tax situation. The bank is completely confused; our correspondences never seem to correspond with the questions they have, things cross in the mail. I guess it will all work out. The bank is too far away to really worry about it. Any reaction we have to anything is so far removed from when something happens in California, it is funny. What seems relevant when I write it, by the time I get your response, I can't remember what question you are answering. All for now.

***

Wednesday, July 5, 1978

Things are starting to settle down. We received all our household baggage, and nothing was broken or missing.

Dear Mom and Dad,
Well, our shipment arrived today. I think everything is here. They did take all our good clothes out of wardrobes and stuffed them in different boxes, so all the suits and good clothes are wrinkled, but they are here. We were thirty pounds underweight, so no taxes. The maid was very helpful today. I think she will work, except she ate my eggs for the chocolate chip cookies, and Super Parmis is out of eggs! The kids are in seventh heaven because all their stuff is here. John met a little boy who has the Star Wars spaceship. John has Obi-Wan, Darth Vader, and some of the other figures, so it is a good combination. Frank Parker hasn't

15

seen Star Wars, so he and John listened to the record and looked at the record jacket pictures. Tori and the girls were really into dressing all the dolls. I haven't figured out what to do with all the kitchen junk. I'm glad I have my little Danish cow, my birds, and ski pictures.

***

Thursday, July 6, 1978

The Fourth of July was not a holiday for us; however, today (our Saturday), we attended the American Fourth of July party held at one of the Tehran American School (TAS) campuses. There must have been several thousand people there. They had a country-and-western band, baseball, skydiving demonstrations, American beer, and American hamburgers and hotdogs. Since we had been here less than a month, it was a great party. For those who had been here for a year or more, it was Christmas, Easter, and Passover all rolled into one. Some spent the whole day eating and drinking. I found out later this was one of the few times we can get American beer.

Dear Mom and Dad,
Today was the Fourth of July celebration at Tehran American School. It was very hot, and it was funny seeing all these Americans standing in line for half an hour for an American hot dog or hamburger. We really haven't been here long enough to appreciate such festivities. When they raised the American flag, thousands of Americans, even kids, stopped and faced the flag and put their hand over their heart, something you don't see too often. It was fun to see shorts, arms, legs, beer cans, blond hair, and no black chadors for a change, and people who understood what you said. But it wasn't the biggest highlight of the trip so far.

***

Friday, July 7, 1978

The Parkers had a big party with swimming and a barbeque. We didn't have any lighter fluid, so Steve cleared the area around the barbeque and the balconies above the barbeque. Once it was cleared, he poured a little gas on the briquettes, stepped back, lit an entire book of matches on fire, and tossed it toward the barbeque. About halfway through the air, there was a small explosion, and the fire was lit! Steve surveyed the area, found it safe, and let the kids return to what they were doing. I put up my American flag, and we all decided to leave it up even after the party.

Dear Mom and Dad,

Well, the American community isn't scoring too well with me. A friend of Claire's, Kathy, told us about a sale at the Pars Club (an American swim and racket club) and told us to use her name and number at the gate. Well, the woman at the gate informed us it was a very private club, and we couldn't enter unless accompanied by a member, and she was the rudest person I have met (British accent). I explained what Kathy told us, and we were only interested in the sale. She could see we didn't have any rackets or swimsuits. So forget that club! We had considered joining before this incident. Kathy called the next day and apologized, saying she was going to complain to the club. John said he had never seen me so mad.

Claire and Steve had a nice Fourth of July swim and dinner party, and we still have the flag up in the backyard. Next year, I think we will let TAS use it. Their flag was ripped and only had forty-eight stars. I hadn't noticed it, but others were mad about it.

***

Saturday, July 8, 1978

Today, I went to work. We now have a telephone and a toilet that flushes. George had fixed some tea, so the day was off to a good start. From the window, I could see the smog creating a brown haze over the city in the distance. Nora has hired a maid who not only cleans but also babysits.

Dear Mom and Dad,

I went shopping with Joan to the big department store for Zhari's shoes (maid). I got some for two hundred rials, and she doesn't like them. *The things one does for a baji. We also went to Tajrishi Bazaar and got some delicious bread and just looked around. Zhari kept the kids, and it sure is nice to come home to a clean house! Claire likes our rug, and Joan thought it was reasonably priced, so we are keeping it. It is a Turkmen tribal rug, 90 percent wool and 10 percent cotton in blues, greens, and browns. It will go in our bedroom at home and is four feet by six feet. What would it cost in the States? We paid three hundred dollars. It is all hand-knotted and colorfast. We still have received no letters in response to our being here.*

***

Sunday, July 9, 1978

Nora went on an ABII hiking trip to sightsee, and she also went shopping at the government stores to price gold and rugs. We purchased our first Persian rug, a Turkmen tribal rug. Four more people from Pacific Bell came since our arrival, and we continue to enjoy our stay as a respite from the "real world."People coming back from vacation in the States say it's more of a culture shock returning to Iran than going back. Nora and I watch a little TV on our one English station, read, play dominoes, and walk.

Dear Mom and Dad,
Today was a real special day. I took the kids on a bus tour, hiking with ABII, and Jean Stevenson had her girls along too. We went to this little village about fifteen minutes from Pahlavi Boulevard, and it was like going back one hundred years. This village had streets so steep and narrow that only donkeys could get through. It was built along the river, and there were many trees. Everything was dark and cool with the sound of rushing water in the background. All the women wore black chadors covering everything but their eyes. All the walls were made of mud bricks with old wooden doors covering entrances off the street. The trees were everywhere—no grass, just the mud walls, wooden doors, donkeys, and the sound of water. Farther up were Iranians camping with a canopy spread over their beautiful rugs laid on the mud banks near the river. As we went farther up, there was a little tea house where we had Cokes, and then there were seven pools where the stream had

been blocked for swimming. It really was picturesque and relaxing. I will bring John here when we get a car.

When we got back to the ABII building, we were met with "Iranian frustrations." A man called cabs for all of us at eleven thirty in the morning, but the other women took all the cabs, leaving Jean and I with four hungry children at twelve thirty, an hour late. A man walked down and called a cab, and his cab was there in five minutes. We went to eat and were ready to leave at one thirty, at which time we were informed they had an extra cab, so we had to take two cabs when one would have sufficed. Oh well.

"During the last 20 years the United States has sold more than $18 billion worth of arms to Iran and has helped organize and equip a vast security system that gives its ruler, Shah Mohammad Reza Pahlavi, absolute control of the country.

In exchange for the support the Shah has committed his country to protect the vital routes out of the Persian Gulf that carry more than half the oil used by Western countries. Furthermore, the income from his arms purchases plus the American technology he buys to help develop his country return to the United States almost $2 annually for every $1 the United States spends on Iranian oil.

The mutually profitable arrangement has forged bonds that are much stronger than American ties to any other developing country. At the same time the relationship has been sharply criticized, both by domestic opponents of the Shah and by Americans, some of them Congress, who condemn his autocratic rule and are fearful that growing Iranian military strength will tempt him into aggressive actions that might drag the United States along."[4]

***

Monday, July 10, 1978

Dear Mom and Dad,

Today was my big day to go on the trip to the bazaar. Zhari was here at seven thirty. I called the cab at seven forty-five. The taxi arrived at *eight twenty. I got to ABII for the bus at eight forty-one, and the bus left at eight forty. This taxi driver was a real "dip," so I didn't want to go to the bazaar alone with him. So I called Claire, who was going to a government handicraft store, and went with her. The government store has regulated prices, so it is a good place to shop. I bought two hand-painted tiles and a hand-painted bud vase for 360 rials or $5.40. It seemed like a real bargain until I converted it to dollars. It was probably more fun than the bazaar anyway. You can't expect anything to be the ultimate here, or you are disappointed that it didn't work out. Claire thought our driver was a pill too.*

I have been playing the guitar a lot and am learning something. We talked to Housing, and we will get credit on the carpet that was missing, so we have enough to make our place look neat. I am going to see the decorator today or tomorrow and get a big machine-made, six-by-fifteen-feet rug for the living room. Our living room and den are thirty feet long and twelve feet wide. This is all marble flooring, a reason I have a cleaning maid or baji. The dining room table seats eight, and we have a four-cushion sofa and four stuffed chairs in the living room, plus a three-cushion couch in the den. It is a big place! Well, that is all for now. I will check the dinner in the Crockpot. It is the first time I have used it.

***

Thursday, July 13, 1978

We played tennis with the Parkers at the Maziar Tennis Club. The Parkers, along with other ABII families, belong to the club, so we joined. It has nine clay courts, six with lights.

***

Friday, July 14, 1978

Today was a highlight day. We took off for a picnic at Darband, an area within Tehran's city limits. As we woke up this morning, we were greeted by a clear, cloudless sky above the mountains. We hiked up to a chair lift, climbed aboard, and were lifted to a lookout restaurant about one thousand feet above the north end of Tehran. Looking back toward the city, all I could see was a smog bank. We continued hiking up from the lookout, passing many little tea houses along the way. I treated Nora, John, and Tori to a glass of freshly squeezed orange juice, and then we continued walking. After about half an hour, we stopped by a little shaded brook for lunch. It was very refreshing, cool, and not crowded. As we were getting up to go, two Iranian women motioned for us to join them for tea. We broke out some of our cookies and shared tea and cookies with them. One spoke fairly good English. She had a son going to school in San Diego and had lived in California herself some time ago. It was a nice stop and very Iranian.

After hiking back down and getting our taxi, which was an hour late, we returned home for a relaxing afternoon of swimming and reading. This evening, the whole family went to church. Church means more over here, and I look forward to going each Friday (our Sunday). I guess being a Catholic in an Islamic country and attending Mass with Americans all rolled into one makes it special.

Last Thursday at the Fourth of July picnic, when playing the American national anthem, you could hear a pin drop. I was greatly impressed, considering there were thousands there, and most were well into their beers. You don't realize what our flag is all about until you're in a foreign country. The Parkers are leaving Tuesday for a six-week vacation. They will be really missed, especially by the kids. We feel very fortunate everything has gone well for us so far. It makes this new experience thoroughly enjoyable.

***

Saturday, July 15, 1978

"President Carter has approved the sale to Iran of nearly $600 million in weapons, including 31 Phantom fighter-bombers, according to Government sources. ...

The proposed sale would be in addition to nearly $2.3 billion in arms already approved for Iran for the 1978 financial year that began last Oct. 1."[5]

***

Sunday, July 16, 1978

We invited the Parkers up for dinner.

Dear Mom and Dad,

The kids are eating fine, and I haven't lost any weight. Thanks, but a case of peanut butter would never make it past customs, and it would have to go by boat to arrive by Christmas. It is available here, so thanks anyway. John's elevator still doesn't work or the air conditioning, but they have toilets and running water sometimes. He gets home at three thirty, which I like, and he finds the job interesting.

We hiked up to Darband for a picnic on Thursday. We rode a chair lift up and walked past all the tea houses and sat by a quiet little mountain stream under the trees. Two Iranian ladies invited us for tea with a cup that leaked until you put two sugar cubes in it. One had a son in San Diego, and the other one's husband and "other wife" were in Israel. Women certainly aren't equals over here, and I have a feeling the only reason people are so nice to me is my "Lady Clairol" blonde hair. Anyway, it was fun, and they were very nice and friendly. On the way down, we had to wait an hour for the taxi while sitting by the jube. This is an open sewer system used to dump garbage in, wash fruits and vegetables, cars, kids' faces, or whatever. It can be bad and smelly, but it is nice and clean where we live. It is the running water, which starts up in the mountains. John called another taxi just before ours pulled up. He waited for the second taxi, which was a white Mercedes (not a Peykan, the Iranian-made car). Everyone we met on the trail said "hi" or "hello," and we said "salaam" (which means peace), and everyone smiled. We saw many people but only two other groups of Americans and no blondes.

***

Monday, July 17, 1978

Dear Mom and Dad,

I took the kids on an ABII tour today to two museums. The paintings from here are neat. They have the delicacy of Oriental art but more substance and aren't too stylized. The faces are all individual noses and expressions. They have horrid oil paintings; it is the little brief sketches and box paintings that are so nice. We also went and saw beautiful little figurines made one thousand years before the birth of Christ, which means that is "old." They are beautiful little things and remind one of the pre-Columbian Inca Indian artifacts. We got two replicas for a thousand rials (about fifteen dollars).

Then, Jean Stevenson and I took the four kids to the American Woman's Club for a pizza. I love their pizzas and Cokes. We had the Parkers for a farewell dinner last night. We had frozen Birds Eye peas (a real treat here), fresh "soft" rolls (most are hard here), Betty Crocker scalloped potatoes (four dollars for two packages), and an Australian roast that I cooked in the Crockpot for fourteen hours with onion soup mix and wine. It was different but very tasty since that meat is usually very dry. It was four pounds for $10.50. The china was nice, and Zhari (our maid) is doing all the dishes this morning.

We joined a tennis club. To play without being a member is twelve dollars an hour. Being a member, it is four dollars an hour and three hundred dollars a year, which is really pretty reasonable. Other clubs were too expensive, and we already have a pool so just needed the tennis.

One more item: I must relate the story of getting the furniture fumigated. We have waited over four weeks now, and finally, they came with a little weed-sprayer can filled with some sort of soap with no odor at all. They dripped all over the floor, and then the sprayer nozzle broke, and the stuff squirted all over like a hose. One guy didn't want to waste the spray, so he put his finger over the end, but it kept spraying while the other one tried to release the pressure. There was stuff on the ceiling, tape deck (which was a good eight feet away), and at least half an inch all over the floor. It was a real Laurel and Hardy comedy. Luckily, the floors are marble, and we had no rugs near this little scene. Today, they are coming back to clean the furniture. I wonder what it will be like. I haven't had time to play bridge over here yet. I'll save that for some "dull times."

I was going to take an oil painting class too, but I will wait on that also. We have TV programs from six to eleven at night. John has been reading instead of watching television. I am nervous to have the Parkers go on vacation. The kids have so much fun together. I'm getting better on the guitar.

***

Tuesday, July 18, 1978

I took the family to the Evin Hotel for dinner and the movie *Russian Roulette*, starring George Segal.

***

Thursday, July 20, 1978

Nora and I played tennis (she won four games in one hour) then went to a softball game. Nora likes the tennis courts here; they are clay and slower. We watched Mike Terry and Terry Scott play, and both were from Pac Bell. We went to their house for dinner, and what a dinner it was. Dave Benfer lives with Mike and Terry. Dave is an excellent cook, and he displayed his talents by serving pork, stuffed chicken, mashed potatoes, two different kinds of gravy, and wine. It was our best meal since our arrival.

***

Friday, July 21, 1978

Today, Gordon and I played tennis. We were evenly matched and split sets; 7–5, 6–4.We played from eleven to twelve thirty but finally had to stop due to the heat. Gordon brought his family over for dinner and swimming. His wife Joan and Nora are looking into a trip to the Greek Islands in the fall. They are great people, and we would enjoy sharing the experience with them. John and Tori are coping well since the Parker kids left for vacation. They will be gone six weeks. Nora is busy going on tours and shopping. Between buying things and going on trips, we will probably net zero financially for the next two years. Next weekend, we get a car, so we will do a little sightseeing outside of Tehran. We will probably visit the ski areas just to get the lay of the land

and see how it goes traveling around at high elevations. We have been here six weeks and still like it.

The following is a letter from son John to Nora's parents:

Dear Grandma and Grandpa,

I like it here very much. It is fun. We have a swimming pool, and downstairs, we have some friends, but they went to the United States for six weeks. And then they will come back. They have two dogs and two cats. Each one of our rooms has one balcony, but the front room does not. There is a range of mountains. They are north, so you will not get lost. We live right next to an American store called Super Parmis. And the food is very different over here. The TV shows are great. But the problem is that TV does not start until seven o'clock, and on the weekend, it starts at noon or one, and sometimes it starts at four. And do you know what they do with sheep? They go on a sidewalk and kill them, and then they butcher them on the sidewalk and bring them and sell them to people. I know so much Farsi. I can say lots of things. It is fun to know Farsi. I have lots of friends. I even know some Iranian friends.

Love, John

***

Sunday, July 23, 1978

Mike Terry, Terry Scott, Dave Benfer, and another couple came over for dinner. Nora fixed some excellent lasagna. We swam, sampled a little Iranian wine, and had a great time.

The early workday and the long daylight gave us almost another day of relaxation after work.

***

Monday, July 24, 1978

Had dinner with John Noske. He is staying at the Parkers' place, cat-sitting.

The following is a letter from son John to my parents:

Dear Ema and Epa,

I miss you very much. I love TV over here. It is neat. They have shows that they do not have in the States. I am reading a book 187 pages long. It is called *The Boy Biggles*. It is the best book I have ever read!!!And about these Star Wars action figures, I only want three or four of them: Death Star Squad Commander, Luke, and Han Solo, and maybe Chewbacca. I would love it if you could get them. I have some already. I like them very much!!!I like Iran. It is fun to learn Farsi. I know lots of words in Farsi. Some of them are salaam, which is hello. And hair is *moo*. No is *nah*. Blue is *ahbee*. Brother is *baradar*. Sister is *khahar*. I know lots of other Farsi too. I live near a store called Super Parmis. It is an American store. Everybody there speaks English. I like our house very much.

Love, John

***

Thursday, July 25, 1978

We went to the Evin American Officer's Club for dinner and invited Terry Scott to go with us. We had pizza, hamburgers, and salad (a real treat). We then went to the ABII free movie, which showed John Wayne in *The Alamo*.

***

Wednesday, July 26, 1978

I picked up a company car to use for the upcoming weekend. The air force sent me an exchange pass that's good until October 1, 1978, so Nora was able to visit the Military Base Exchange. She bought toys for the kids and American liquor (Johnnie Walker Red Label for $4.25) for us. She was able to stock up in anticipation of not being able to get any liquor for the next two years. Nora made a beautiful macramé to hang in our living room. She has adjusted quickly since our arrival. We just heard our local Farsi class starts Monday.

Dear Mom and Dad,

I just got back from a tour of the Golestan Palace with a bunch of mothers. We left twelve kids at one house with three sitters (I'm glad it wasn't my house) and took off on a bus. The kids had fun, and we had fun by ourselves. We came home to a nice clean house (Zhari, our cleaner, had been there). John came home, and now I am at the Hilton waiting to get my haircut. I hate snooty beauty shops, and this place sure seems that way. Everyone is getting their toenails painted and getting rollers and eyebrow "somethings." All I want is a good blunt haircut, and I haven't seen a pair of scissors since I came in here. Today, the taxi was early, so I have half an hour to wait. (After the haircut.) Well, I got a good haircut, and ladies talked about me, but I have no idea what they said. I guess I'll go back in six weeks.

We went to the officer's club for dinner and saw John Wayne in The Alamo. *Socially, we have been very busy. Thursday, we went to Terry Scott and his two roommates' for dinner. Friday, we had John's boss and family over to swim and for dinner and to play tennis. Saturday, I went to the Golestan Palace, and then Sunday, I went on a tour of the Pahlavi Palace followed by having two kids and eight adults for lasagna. Monday night, we went out to dinner and Tuesday to the officer's club. So we have been busy. Next weekend, Raj Madhok gets a minibus, and we hope to go to the Caspian. John gets his first car this weekend.*

The most exciting thing is I got in the military co-op and bought a hundred dollars' worth of California wine, liquors, bourbon whiskey, light beer, Excedrin, and toys for the kids. A bottle of Kahlúa was $4.50! I guess there is no tax. I was so excited; triple sec is $3.50, a gallon of tequila is $3.50, one quart of Scotch is $4.50.Tennis balls are $4.50.It was a real treat to get into the base exchange.

I have a maid three days a week. It is a real luxury. She does everything, and I sit and write letters. She costs ten dollars, while a jar of mayonnaise is twelve dollars, one hour of tennis for non-members at the club is twelve dollars—so it's a deal! Once she leaves, we do find things in weird places. All my shorts are with John's, my tennis socks are in Tori's room, and my Crockpot cookbook was in Tori's toy closet. The kids panic every time she comes because she puts things in strange places, so their rooms are always clean. I "panicked" because I couldn't find the basket for my plants. Zhari had tried to throw it away before, and I said no, so now I found it under John's bed. Our shipment of things all arrived unbroken except they used our good clothes, like suits, to stuff in the boxes. I just finished a four-foot-by-two-foot macramé hanging and am getting better on the guitar.

I have been going on lots of tours. The palaces, jewels, rugs, mosaics, and art are absolutely fantastic. There is one palace with an entire room made of pieces of chipped mirror, including the ceiling, with the largest handmade rug in the world. Another room is entirely inlaid wood, including the doorknobs, curtain rods, desk, doors, everything. It took eight years to build using twenty men or something like that. We have bought one rug and a ruby ring so far.

***

Thursday, July 27, 1978

"An Iran Air Boeing 727 jetliner with a jammed landing gear made a crash landing at Teheran Airport early today, but none of the 65 people aboard was injured."[6]

***

Friday, July 28, 1978

We had a car yesterday and today, so we did a lot of driving. Yesterday, we headed east into the mountains to a town called Farshah and had a picnic by a stream flowing down from the snow high in the mountains. We attended a party last night with Terry Scott, Mike Terry, and about thirty of their friends. It was very nice with an excellent buffet. Today, we drove out west to the town of Karaj, which was a lot flatter and hotter but still very interesting. The rest of the night was spent quietly at home.

Son John started a Star Wars jigsaw puzzle, with me doing most of it. I finished another book by Ludlum: *The Gemini Contenders*. Next weekend, we are supposed to go to the Caspian with the Madhoks. I

28

understand it has been very crowded lately, so we are not sure yet if we will go or not.

***

Saturday, July 29, 1978

"Iran's Health Minister reported today that cholera had broken out in a central desert town and at a Persian Gulf port.

Nasrollah Mojdehi, who was appointed Health Minister on Monday, said in a broadcast: 'The disease is under full control. There is no cause for alarm.'

He said six persons had died in Gonabad, 528 miles *east* of Teheran. A newspaper reported that eight persons had died there.

The Health Minister made no mention of deaths in Minab, a port 932 miles south, of Teheran."[7]

***

Monday, July 31, 1978

Dear Mom and Dad,

Well, we had a car this past weekend and set off for unknown adventures. The first thing I did was lose the map! We drove along a river on the way up to Shemshak, a ski area, to have a picnic near a stream. The hills are so bleak and barren and look worse than California during a drought. It is the only land I have seen that man can improve upon. They have vast reforestation programs all over and many military bases. Thursday night (our Saturday), we went to a party at Mike Terry, Terry Scott, and Dave Benfer's house. Then Friday, we set off in another direction toward Karaj. We passed a beautiful new sports stadium and athlete village, which is seldom used. Our picnic consists of cheese, German crackers, Cokes, fruit, and peanut butter.

I have been looking into converting some money into Swiss francs, as the rial is momentarily holding up the dollar at false prices. I got all the info I need; I just need to convince John. The bank is right downtown, and I know enough now to actually question the taxi drivers as to their route. Some of them love to go through traffic instead of the expressway. I left the kids with Zhari and was going to the base exchange, but it was closed. I wanted to stock up on wine and toys before September 30th. A bottle of California wine is a treasured item around here. They are nice for dinner, promotion, and going away gifts. I've had such good success at the base exchange that I tried the commissary yesterday. The kids get so excited about the funniest things: big red apples, tomato soup, maple syrup, lettuce, and cookies. So I loaded up but couldn't check out because my military pass doesn't qualify for the commissary. Just the exchange. The food shopping was a waste of time!

The kids have really settled down. They don't tease and fight so much. Tori is playing dress-up and hiding her blonde hair under her chador and going shopping by crossing the jube with her shopping basket full of plastic bags. Son John is taping everything on the radio. Today, Zhari saw me putting paper on the kitchen shelves, so she cleaned the top of the refrigerator and put newspaper on top of it (first time the refrigerator top has been cleaned). I went to a lot of work to find other clients for Zhari, but she won't work for less than fifteen dollars a day; she only charges me ten dollars. I don't understand why she won't take on more work but feel fortunate to have her.

I guess our trip to the Caspian is canceled, as no one will confirm the reservations for the weekend. In Iran, if someone has a room, they can keep it as long as they want as long as they pay. So reservations are kind of meaningless. Also, this time of year, many from the southern provinces are flocking to the Caspian, a reason to stay away. I'm desperate to see a large body of water with boats on it. We may try Karaj dam for the day or something similar. Things here are very indefinite.

I went to the big bazaar on Saturday, and it was really fun. I purchased another gold chain (a good investment over here), a hand-painted pencil box, camel bells for my macramé, and an Esfahan print hat for John to wear while skiing. The bazaar wasn't as big, scary, dirty, or exotic as I had thought it would be. I guess I've gotten used to most things here. The city is getting dustier, though, as it hasn't rained for six weeks.

***

Tuesday, August 1, 1978

"The Government today confirmed that seven people were killed, dozens injured and more than 300 arrested in anti-government riots in 13 towns in the last week.

A spokesman said the casualty figures, which reported by newspapers, were accurate. But he denied claims by a Moslem priest that 40 people were killed in a riot in Meshed 10 days ago and said the priest had since corrected his figures to one dead and 30 injured.

The riots were apparently sparked by religious fervor, whipped up by elements opposed to the Shah's secular rule, at mourning ceremonies for two religious leaders who died early this month, one in a car crash, the other of natural causes."[8]

***

Thursday, August 3, 1978

I played tennis with Gordon, and Nora played tennis with Joan. I secured a car for three days.

***

Friday, August 4, 1978

We drove to the Tochal skiing chairlift for a picnic. Once we left Tehran proper and drove just a little, we were in desolate mountains and valleys. The mountains had little vegetation, but the valleys were usually green with growth and areas where people lived. Gordon brought a six-pack of beer. We hiked around the area and then returned to get our lunch out of the car. It was all there except for the six-pack. The car had been locked. We looked all around but never solved the disappearing beer mystery.

***

Saturday, August 5, 1978

The holy month of Ramadan begins.

Dear Mom and Dad,
Today is the first day of Ramadan. The religious Muslims don't eat or drink anything from sunup to sunset for thirty days, and some of them beat themselves with chains as a test to their faith. When I called the taxi company, they wanted to know where I was going. They sent me a nice young cab driver. This past weekend, the embassy asked everyone to stay out of the bazaar and public Iranian spots as they predict trouble. Was there any? You would hear before we would. I went to the embassy this morning and stocked up on California wines, beer, liquor, and Lego toys. I had to return all the tennis balls, as they are pressurized, and we need high-altitude, unpressurized balls, or the ball bounces all over the place.
This past weekend was a three-day holiday, and we wanted to go to the Caspian Sea, but we couldn't get any reservations. On Thursday (our Saturday), we played tennis. I played with Joan Griffes, and John played with Gordon. Terry Scott was nice enough to give us his car this weekend. Friday, the family went to Tochal on the new chairlift with the Griffeses and their two girls. We fit eight in one car when it was ninety-five degrees. The ski lift goes up for miles, and when it is completed, it will connect Tehran with the best ski area in the world. It was really fun. We hiked with our coolers from the top and descended to a valley where you couldn't see anything but barren mountains; no Iranians, no people, no trees, no grass, no water—nothing but rocks, shale, strange plants, wildflowers, and lizards the size of your foot. The kids practiced shouting echoes in the canyon and throwing rocks. It was fun to get away from everything. I had put a stew in the Crockpot before leaving, so dinner was ready when we got home. Joan brought over potatoes, so we had potato salad, watermelon, and brownies. We ate by the pool and left all the dirty dishes for Zhari the next day. Following dinner, we played a little bridge.
Today, the holiday, we went on a picnic with the Corricellos and another family in an Iranian orchard. She is American, and her husband Mohammad is an Iranian, and they have two children, one year and two years old. Mohammad owns the apple orchard in Karaj. All the children

had a great time running within the trees and grass. We picked huge apples, which I used to make my first apple pie from scratch! After spending time in the orchard, we returned for our Farsi class. The instructor was an hour late due to traffic from the Caspian. We learned to count to one million. I'm not sure we will continue these classes after this miniclass. We are taking the class with a nice couple who have two kids and live down the street. The other day, I was supposed to go on a tour, but it was canceled. I joined another lady with her kids, and we all shopped for gold. I got my John another gold chain—seventeen karats, four and a half grams, Iranian gold—for twenty-seven dollars. We looked around a week ago, and the price of gold was six dollars a gram; today, it was $8.75. School starts September 2nd. John went to bed at 9:30p.m.; he gets up at 5:45a.m. every morning, so he gets tired.

"Shah Mohammad Reza Pahlavi announced today his personal commitment to free elections and liberalized political life within the law.

'We will give political freedom as in the democratic countries,' the Shah said in a broadcast, 'and as in the democratic countries, the limits of this freedom will be fixed.'

The Shah, in a speech to mark the anniversary of the establishment of constitutional monarchy in Iran in 1906, indicated that there would be no major changes in the political process before elections for Parliament set for next June. But he confirmed that laws would be enacted to govern freedom of political meetings and of the press, as previously announced by the Government."[9]

***

Sunday, August 6, 1978

I have been put totally in charge of the Status Room for the Imperial Commission (the Shah's Board of Directors). August 15 is the forecasted completion date, which we are all working hard to meet. The kids are watching *Zorro* on TV—great reruns. Nora is attempting to make an apple pie from scratch for the first time in eleven years.

<u>ABII Notice</u>

"Ramadan, the Moslem month of fasting and meditation, begins today, August 6th, and continues until September 3rd. It is a time when Moslems, those who are physically able, refrain from eating, drinking, and smoking from sunrise to sunset.

For Moslems, it is a time of prayer and meditation; a time to rest and purify the body; and a time to truly feel the plight of those who regularly go hungry and thirsty in the world, so that hearts may be opened to help the needy. …

During Ramadan, some restaurants will be closed. Others will remain open but with paper covering windows so as to avoid offending those who are fasting. This is a time when it is impolite for non-Moslems to smoke or eat on the streets or anywhere in public during the daylight hours."[10]

***

Tuesday, August 8, 1978

We went to the Evin Hotel with Terry Scott to see *The Man with the Golden Gun*.

***

Thursday, August 10, 1978

"Iran's army, backed by tanks and armored cars, seized control of Iran's ancient capital of Isfahan today and declared a dusk-to-dawn curfew to end 18 hours of arson and pillage by hundreds of Moslem extremists.

The U.S. consulate in Isfahan told the approximately 12,000 Americans in the city to stay indoors until further notice.

Tanks, armored cars and personal vehicles filled with soldiers moved into the streets of Isfahan, 257 miles south of Tehran, after clashes throughout the night and before noon today.

There were reports of an undetermined number of deaths and injuries in the rioting.

Major General Reza Naji, military commander of the region, took command in the city of blue domes, covered Persian bazaars and lush boulevards after martial law was declared today.

The army moved in after riot police failed to control hundreds of anti-shah religious demonstrators who rampaged through the city burning banks and shops.

Isfahan is a major steel and industry center. The Americans mostly are involved with civil projects and a few defense-related industries being built there by Iran's government.

The riot erupted as the shah, in the first interview with resident foreign correspondents of his reign, warned extremists they would be crushed if they attempted to block his moves toward political liberalization."[11]

"Authorities in Tehran said that four rioters were killed and seven wounded when police opened fire to quell the antigovernment demonstrations…Seven policemen suffered bullet wounds and 38 others were injured by flying rocks and bricks, they said.

The rioters attacked and set fire to a big luxury hotel, smashed the windows of banks and movie theaters, damaged cars, and attacked fire engines, injuring 40 firemen, they said.

The scale of the rioting appeared to be the biggest yet in a wave of protests against the government of Shah Mohammad Reza Pahlavi throughout the country this year."[12]

**

Friday, August 11, 1978

It was a weekend of tennis, swimming, horse races, and more tennis. We all just got home from evening Mass. I will be following the selection of a new pope closely. Tonight, we had lettuce! It has been almost two months since lettuce has been available. Nora mixed up some Green Goddess salad dressing to celebrate the occasion. Last night, we had the Sozzis (my former ABII boss) over for dinner, an excellent meal of hamburgers, potato salad, and cake. Nora is cooking better meals here than when we were in Pleasant Hill, California. After eating, we went to the horse races at a nearby stadium. The facilities were very nice, including a beautiful building that housed the stables. There was no grass in the field, and the course was rough. The horses ran in the opposite direction than American racehorses. The clientele was very clean and well dressed—so, not in the typical American fashion of shorts and flip-flops. Our net loss amounted to sixty rials or about nine dollars.

I played doubles with Terry Scott over the weekend and split sets. Gordon and I played John Noske and his son today; we lost, so we have to fix them dinner next Friday. I'm definitely playing more tennis. Unfortunately, it's just not better tennis. Nora is playing up to twice a week, though, and getting better.

Tomorrow, the Status Room for the generals should be finished. The Imperial Commission is due to visit August 15. I hope everything is to their liking, or I may be going home sooner than expected. I helped design and furnish the Status Room and even purchased an Iranian flag with a pedestal for the room and a huge conference table (six-foot-by-twelve-foot long).But my main job was gathering the data and deciding what to show and what not to show the generals. We ended up deciding to show them everything so there are no surprises.

Nora is helping Tori learn to read, while John is doing fourth grade math (he goes into third grade in September).

***

Saturday, August 12, 1978

With little TV, we have lots of time to write letters, read, and listen to music. Iran would be the perfect country for investors in solar energy; the sun is out at least 80 percent of the year. A week ago, the Iranians started Ramadan, a thirty-day holy season. From four to eight, they can't have any food, water, smokes, etc. And we Catholics think we have it hard with Lent. The auto accident rate seems to be going up toward the end of the day—lots of empty stomachs and short tempers.

Dear Mom and Dad,

I'm sure you have heard about the riots in Isfahan. We are fine here, but we are "in" Ramadan, a holy period, which is not a very happy time, and August 26 is supposed to be a very sad time. So far, we haven't seen anything out of the ordinary. We went to the horse races Thursday night, and there were soldiers but no problems. On the way home, traffic was stopped by three buses cutting across all the lanes. One was stalled and another was pushing it. The cars kept cutting in front of the buses and around them, which made "progress" difficult. Some drove across dividers on the wrong side of the street, honking. We were driving in a big Blazer, which was "above" all the traffic and events.

Last night, we had blue cheese dressing on our salad. I brought some packets from the States; when mixed with mayonnaise and butter milk, it makes salad dressing. Maybe you could send us some more of these packets. I think they were from Pay and Save or Payless and were very cheap, twenty cents.

Today, I went with Rene Corricello and some other mothers and kids to a park at the foot of a mountain. Son John and two other boys climbed to the top all by themselves. They had a regular rooting section of Iranians watching them from the bottom. One mother took a picture, and I will try to get a copy.

Our local magazine, Dear ABII, *had a photo contest, and we won fourth place with a picture of Tori with a ski hat, taken when she was small in Pleasant Hill. She will be in the quarterly magazine! We called it "Patriotic Beauty."Right now, Tori is playing "having the right color pass to get into the commissary" with her bus and little stuffed animals/people. John is in his room because the neighbors complained about the noise from his radio during Ramadan during fasting and nap time.*

Tehran American School starts August 27.John thinks the kids should go to Piruzi, an international school, but it may be too late. And besides, it starts a week later. I think John needs the after-school sports that TAS offers, maybe not tackle football but soccer. I looked into a correspondence course through Ohio University. I might also work, but I'm not quite ready yet. We don't need the money, and ABII doesn't offer challenging jobs for spouses. The Parkers will be back either this week or next. We need to straighten this out because we are the ones who need to pick them up at the airport. We have played lots of tennis, and everyone is healthy. (Later)I called Piruzi. The Parkers and everyone I know is sending their kids there. If they pass the entrance test, I guess John and Tori will go also. I found out TAS has some issues (perhaps drugs), and they still haven't called me to ask what grades the kids are in and where we live so the school can put the kids on their bus route. Piruzi asked for the kids' birthdays, who recommended them, where they used to go to school, and John's work telephone number. And this was all to just take the entrance test. I also saw a notebook of a TAS student, and it looked worse than John's papers and spelling. So, we shall see.

Send political articles; no one censors them. I am curious what the U.S. says about Shiraz and Isfahan. The Shah is a great U.S. friend. He keeps his currency stable, based on the dollar. I think all the problems here are communist inspired. Iranians are gentle people, short tempered but not vicious. We don't have military protection from Germany anymore. I guess we will forget Spain and focus on Greece for our vacation this year.

***

Sunday, August 13, 1978

Dear Mom and Dad,

We received your newsy letter of July 28.Thank you. First, surprising news: we are sending the kids to an international school instead of the American school. They will go to Piruzi. It is where the Stevensons, Madhoks, Corricellos, and Parkers are all sending their kids. There is a maximum of twenty kids to a class. They took an entrance exam, which they both passed with flying colors, except I didn't give Tori any breakfast and let her sleep before the test, which amazed the teacher. We have at least ten pages of forms to fill out on both of them. Tori's test was around twenty minutes and John's was over one hour, but he said it was easy. I had called Tehran American School in July, and they told me to call in August. I called August 2, and they set up a test for Tori on August 21.Then I found out school starts August 27, and the bus schedule was to come out August 23.How could they get teachers qualified in classes, buses, and textbooks if they don't try and get a preliminary enrollment? John was also upset that they let the kids John's age play tackle football. So...Piruzi!

We are considering a trip to Greece and the islands at the end of September. Isn't there someplace we could see you, like Athens or something? We are planning September 24 to October 3 as it stands right now. I think we will take a boat tour for seven days. We will leave the kids here. They will be settled in school and be gone from seven thirty to three, so I don't think they will miss us too much. Probably, we will be in Athens September 24 and October 1 and 2. We could see the Acropolis together. Let us know if it would work. We can be sort of flexible. It is past the tourist season, so I don't think we will have problems with reservations. Please send us some envelopes of salad dressing. Ready-made is three dollars, and we are able to get lettuce now.

Tomorrow is John's big day with his orientation room. All the vendors came through except ABII, and they won't pay for the displays. He is usually home at three, and it is after four. He isn't home yet—troubles. It is an ABII problem, nothing to do with the Iranians. Well, John just got home at five with another tale about Iran. He finally got the check for the displays from ABII. The truck they sent to pick up the displays had no ropes and looked like an open cattle truck, so John and five men stood in the back of the truck in his suit pants and tie, keeping the displays from hitting each other, driving through Tehran traffic. As the truck drove down the streets, people looked, pointed, and laughed. His tie and hair were blowing in the wind, but it was successful in delivering the boards intact and undamaged. The five men had to take the five-foot-by-six-foot displays up seven flights of fire escapes while John went up the elevator with ten smaller displays. So today, the general should come to review the project. I think it is neat that they gave John a job to complete by a certain date, and he did it!

You heard about the riots in Isfahan no doubt. We hear things but don't see any problems. I can't help but think it is communist subversion causing all the troubles. Iranians have short tempers and will yell, but they certainly don't seem very violent or like an angry mob.

"A bomb exploded in a crowded luxury restaurant in the Iranian capital…killing one person and injuring 45, including about 10 Americans, police reported…

The dead man was an Iranian who police suspect was carrying the bomb into the basement of the Khansalaar restaurant.

None of the Americans was hurt seriously, a U.S. Embassy official said. About 20 other persons remained hospitalized with serious injuries.

Iranian troops have been on alert in major cities since a new round of anti-government demonstrations by Moslem conservatives began last week. Officials said they doubted, however, that the blast involved guerrilla action linked to the demonstration. No group claimed responsibility."[13]

***

Tuesday, August 15, 1978

The Status Room is finally finished. We are ready for visitors to review the status of the ABII-TCI partnership.

***

Wednesday, August 16, 1978

The family went to the Evin Hotel in the evening to watch the movie *Old Dracula*, starring David Niven. I also got a haircut.

One incident we found was interestingly dealt with was a bicycle accident. It was late in the afternoon when we noticed a crowd gathering at a corner. We approached, and it appeared a bicycle rider had been hit by a car driven by a foreigner. The bike rider was on the ground crying out in pain. Anger at the driver was starting to rise, when an Iranian gentleman, dressed in a nice suit, walked up and asked if he could help. The driver explained that the bike appeared out of nowhere, and the car hit it. The gentleman knelt by the bike rider and spoke to him. He then told the driver if he could pay the "hurt" rider the equivalent of thirty dollars in rials, all would be fine. The driver paid the bike rider, who then got up, took his bike, and walked away a few thousand rials richer. None of us knew if it was rigged or was just the way things were handled over here.

THE UNDOING

Saturday, August 19, 1978

We had the Parkers and Webster Van De Mark for dinner. He was from Bell Labs and had a very interesting background, including motion picture director, combat photographer, author (of numerous novels), art teacher in college, and is working on his doctorate. He is also a movie buff, and I enjoyed discussing old movies with him. Conversation centered on what today's headlines mean for our project.

"HOLOCAUST! 377 Burned alive in Abadan Cinema Arson.

An Abadan cinema was turned into a human holocaust Saturday night when 377 men, women, and children were burnt alive by arsonists in what ranks among the worst terrorist acts in history.

The exact number of survivors was still unclear, but officials said 10 people were hospitalized with critical burns and only about 40 people escaped unharmed.

Government spokesmen blamed the arson on saboteurs and religious extremists."[14]

"At least six times in the previous ten days, anti-government members of Iran's conservative Shi'ite Muslim sect and other groups had attacked movie theaters in protest against the religious and social liberalization policies of Shah Mohammad Reza Pahlavi. Late last week, in what could well be one of the most destructive terrorist assaults in recent history, the fanatics struck again. Some 400 mostly young Iranians were jammed into the Rex Cinema in Abadan, an oil refining center some 450 miles south of Tehran, to watch a local film production, *The Deer*. Terrorists poured jet fuel around the building, and without warning set it on fire. At least 377 people were burned alive; only a handful managed to escape to the roof and jump to safety. Ironically, the house manager of the Rex himself had locked the theater doors earlier to protect customers from a terrorist assault; only two months ago a bomb had exploded at the Rex at a time when no one was there."[15]

"Most of the victims appeared to have suffocated or were trampled in the stampede to escape.
'The cries of help were so pathetic that I could die hearing them,' one witness said. 'There were hundreds watching a disaster taking place, but they could do little to prevent it.'
The theater's only exit was locked. ...
Rescuers demolished walls to get inside, but found the floor already littered with limbs 'burned to charcoal.' Some collapsed in hysteria at the sight."[16]

***

Sunday, August 20, 1978

With the finishing of the Status Room on August 15, we have now started updating the information, which is a continuous process. This past weekend, Gordon and I played tennis and treated John Noske and his son to dinner at our place (since they won last week). We cooked and served, all for ninety dollars. What a meal it was: chips, dips, American beer, Paul Masson wine, shrimp, Australian top sirloin steak, green salad with Green Goddess dressing, potato salad, and cake! The meat itself was twenty-five dollars. So, while things are not cheap here, we can still eat well.

Last Friday, I reserved a minibus and went out to the airport to pick up the Parkers from their vacation. It's nice to have them back, and they are glad to be back, if you can believe that. Steve turned down a job with his "home" company while he was back there. I hope they stay as long as we do. We had the Parkers over for dinner last night, along with our bachelor work friend Webster.

Today, I shaved off my mustache. Our eleventh anniversary is just around the corner, August 26, and as a gift to ourselves, we'll be going on a trip to Greece with the Griffeses in September. The kids start school September 6. We are sending them to Piruzi, an international school, instead of Tehran American School. We feel an international education, learning about different cultures and meeting people from all over the world, is more appropriate.

ABII Security

"The following alert has been issued by the United States Embassy. As a general precautionary step in respect of the deep mourning days of the *4.5[Muslim] holy month of Ramadan from August 24 through August 27, and on August 31, United States Mission personnel and the American community should maintain the lowest profile possible, refraining from participating in tours, hosting or attending large parties, festivities, and other forms of overt activity. Americans should avoid, during this period of time, areas of the city such as bazaars, mosques, university areas, and installations such as restaurants, banks, movie theatres, etc., where incidents of civil disorder have occasionally occurred."[17]

***

Monday, August 21, 1978

"The country is facing what the Shahanshah has called 'the Great Terror,' Minister of Information and Tourism Dariush

Homayoun said…

Speaking after a cabinet meeting, Homayoun said the kind of barbarism seen in Abadan on Saturday night was only matched by the barbarism of the Fascist era in Germany. …

Asked about the likelihood of imposing martial law on Shiraz and Abadan where terrorist activity has been on the increase, Homayoun said the Government could defeat terrorism and subversion without resorting to martial law.

He assured further security measures would be taken to protect public and private property and there was no reason for panic."[18]

***

Tuesday, August 22, 1978

"More than 10,000 people mourning the death of the Rex Cinema fire victims went wild with grief at Abadan Cemetery…

Men, women and children poured earth on their heads and writhed around in the dust in scenes that even shocked and sickened hardened detectives and veteran crime reporters.

Scores of ambulances, on stand-by to rush those overcome by grief to hospital, were very busy throughout the sorrowful ceremony."[19]

***

Wednesday, August 23, 1978

We went to the Evin Hotel with Terry Scott for dinner and a movie, which was *Thief*.

***

Thursday, August 24, 1978

There have been some incidents in the southern part of the country due to the Abadan fire.

Swam in the pool and read today. Nora and I played tennis in the evening.

ABII Notice

"Three of the saddest days in the Moslem year occur this week and next, on August 24th, 25th, and 26th. …

These three days and especially the 26th are a time of sorrow for Moslems. Radio and television will be curtailed, and many restaurants and places of recreation will be closed. For foreign visitors in Iran, it is a time to be sensitive to religious feelings of those around us. Keep a low profile and avoid giving offense by such things as playing loud music and wearing bright clothing."[20]

***

Friday, August 25, 1978

We played tennis with the Griffeses. This evening, we stayed up late and talked to the Parkers about our future in Iran. While Steve and his family have been in Iran longer than us, he has not seen demonstrations or riots up to this point. We both felt the unrest could make the working conditions more difficult, but we decided to take a "wait and see" attitude.

***

Saturday, August 26, 1978

It is our eleventh wedding anniversary. All the recent problems are the result of religious and political tensions. For instance, many are upset about the movie theaters, restaurants, and bars that have not closed during Ramadan, and the Abadan fire that killed 377 is a tragic example of that anger. Today, we are to maintain a low profile because it's a "sad/serious" day of mourning in Islam. We try to keep the kids quiet; we are reading much more over here than we did in the U.S. At least the Status Room is finished.

***

Sunday, August 27, 1978

Prime Minister Jamshid Amouzegar resigned after being in office one year and twenty days. Could this be the first sign something "unsettling" is on the horizon?

***

Monday, August 28, 1978

TCI executives visited our Status Room. They seemed satisfied with our progress and the status of various projects.

Jafar Sharif-Emami was named the new prime minister by the Shah today. He is more conservative and the grandson of a Muslim leader, which may help the Shah bridge those in favor of his reform programs with those who are more focused on religious principles.

***

Tuesday, August 29, 1978

ABII Notice

"Monday, September 4,1978, is a religious holiday and because of the present situation, will be observed by ABII. All ABII and TCI offices will be closed. Arrangements will be made to inform all employers of contract employees that they will not be expected to report to work and will be paid.

For security reasons, it is suggested that employees and their dependents keep a low profile and stay away from crowded places such as the bazaar and universities."[21]

***

Thursday, August 31, 1978

Played tennis with Nora. We then had the Griffeses over for dinner and bridge.

There is less night life in Tehran now, and the atmosphere is subdued. Many of the cinemas here and around the country have closed as the holy month of Ramadan comes to an end and due to the fire in Abadan.

***

Friday, September 1, 1978

Nora and I played tennis.

***

Sunday, September 3, 1978

I played tennis last night with Steve Parker under the lights. The courts were completely lit, and we both played well.

Today is the last day of Ramadan, the month of fasting. Tomorrow has been declared a holiday, so we are going on an early morning hike with the Corricellos up Kolec Chow to a camp three thousand feet behind Tehran and then returning for dinner at the Parkers with Jim Turner. Tomorrow is also Tori's fifth birthday, but we aren't going to celebrate it until the fifth, just a little party with eleven friends. While we're definitely going to Greece, we still are not sure of the dates. We will leave either September 20 or September 27, depending on the availability of cruise tours. Nora and I are looking forward to this; it will be our first trip without children, an eleven-year delayed honeymoon.

***

Monday, September 4, 1978

Today, we celebrated Labor Day, so no work. We hiked up to Kolec Chow with the Corricellos. It was a desolate area, and once we reached the destination, there were tents for camping and a place where we could get some bean soup. The air was clean up there, but while looking back toward Tehran, I could see the smog hanging over the city.

***

Tuesday, September 5, 1978

Had Tori's birthday party with some of her friends.

***

Wednesday, September 6, 1978

Today, I started working directly with the military on reporting progress on the Seek Switch Program. I was impressed with the caliber of officers in the army. Gatherings in public places were banned. Despite that, we joined the Parkers for Piruzi school night followed by dinner at the Evin Hotel. The classes at Piruzi would be taught in English, but in the schoolyard, the kids would be able to speak in any of their languages: Italian, Russian, German, French, etc. We were shown the playground, which was actually under the building.

***

Thursday, September 7, 1978

There were huge demonstrations in Tehran.

***

Friday, September 8, 1978

During the last six months, the Shah has been having problems with religious groups who think he has moved Iran too fast and too far into the twentieth century, which has led to more and more demonstrations and riots throughout the country. Up to this weekend, the disturbances were tolerated by the Shah because of the pressure exerted by President Carter and his human rights policy. However, the Shah ran out of patience after the riots hit Tehran over the weekend. He declared martial law in Tehran this morning and imposed a curfew from nine at night to five in the morning. The army quickly moved into position to deal with the disturbances. Deciding to call the Shah's bluff, demonstrators marched late this morning, but the army opened fire and killed ten to twenty people and wounded another one hundred. Many fires have erupted around the city. All airline flights due to depart or arrive after nine at night have been rescheduled, and movie theaters, bars, restaurants, and night clubs closed early. The army is everywhere; they are very effective and efficient. The last time Iran had trouble of this magnitude was in 1953 when the CIA prevented the Shah's overthrow. The rumor mill is running on full power!

We had the Madhoks, Corricellos, and Parkers for dinner. That could be the last dinner for some time. Tori and John start school tomorrow, September 9. Both are very excited. Nora and I are doing our best to downplay what's going on in the country so as not to worry them. They both enjoy Tehran so much and have made so many friends; we don't want to spoil it.

Just heard the news at ten: fifty-eight are dead and 205 were wounded in the demonstrations. Martial law has been imposed for six months. We are well protected in northern Tehran; the army is thick around the Shah's palace. All that is necessary is to obey the law and stay away from the "hot spots."

"MARTIAL LAW

The Government declared dusk-to-dawn curfew in Tehran and 11 other cities for six months following Thursday's massive demonstrations in defiance of the ban on unauthorized gatherings.

Commander of the Ground Forces General Gholam Aki Oveisi who was made military governor of Tehran and suburbs, declared a curfew from 9 p.m. to 5 a.m. every day. ...

The martial law government announced last night that 58 people were killed and 205 injured according to hospital reports received by 5:30 p.m.

The announcement said that the casualties occurred when armed subversives, financed by foreigners, attacked security forces injuring them. ...

The announcement said the government had to intervene to protect Iran's national identity and unity and the people's social and individual rights which faced very serious threat."[22]

***

Saturday, September 9, 1978

Dear Mom and Dad,

Well, things are business as usual around here, regardless of what it looks and sounds like. Our neighbor next door, who has been there for twenty years, said he was glad the Shah finally stepped in and did something. Last night, we had the Corricellos (four), Madhoks (four), and Parkers (five) for hamburgers. The curfew went into effect, and the Madhoks couldn't get a taxicab to go across town. Luckily, the Corricellos had a car they could use to get home by nine.

Today was the first day of school, and while I am delighted to have the little "dears" out of my hair, I feel sort of useless. The house takes care of itself; the kids are gone from seven to three; the bazaar is closed; taxi drivers won't go downtown—what can I do? I signed up to substitute teach at Piruzi, and the principal called and asked me to teach kindergarten full time 8:00 a.m. to 2:30p.m.I said no. I couldn't stand having little kids that long. I heard of a job teaching English to Iranian Air Force officers for two days a week. I called, but they said the openings were filled. I may do this, but I want to be flexible for trips, the kids, and I don't think I want to do anything fulltime. Besides, I'm not sure I want to be on an air force bus at this particular time.

Claire rode the bus with the kids this morning, and I met her with a cab. There were soldiers with guns and bayonets on the street corners. I put a photocopy of the kids' passports in their lunch boxes and had John memorize our phone number, street directions, and that his dad worked for ABII. Tori knows about ABII and our address: Koocheh Myram #6. On the way home from school, Tori fell asleep on the bus. When everyone got off, minus her, all of them ran after the bus yelling for it to stop. Finally, all were reunited and walked back home.

The biggest thing is to know where your passports are and keeping them up to date with resident permits so you can leave if necessary. We are not real sure about the Greece trip at the moment. We will have to wait and see if things settle down. It really is unreal when I think of California and how it is here. They search my bags at stores for guns and bombs. We had tickets for The Merry Widow *at Ridacci Hall, but it was canceled. There is no eating out, no movies, and no night classes. I'm hoping they will lift the curfew if people behave. I feel like a bad teenager who has been grounded.*

Last Monday was Tori's birthday. We got up at five to join the Corricellos for a hike early in the morning. We had bean soup, bread, and cakes for breakfast. It was fun, and we all made it to the top and back down. Tori was a little tired. The kids each ate a candy bar to celebrate her birthday. Then on Tuesday, we had her birthday party. We are still flying the American flag in our backyard. It is too bad all Americans can't have this experience; they would appreciate all we have more and our system of government, what it stands for, and how it operates. I am usually so opinionated and informed about politics, but having read everything here, talked to people, watched the news—I still can't figure out what and why these demonstrations are happening. The opposition to the Shah is so varied; it seems as if he is in the middle of two radical viewpoints. The only ones who are benefiting from all these demonstrations are the Muslim Marxists, who delight in chaos. The Iranian Army is trained by some branch of the Israel Army, so they are good and efficient. Things are peaceful when they are around with their bayonets out. The opposition can't hold meetings of more than two people, nor are they supposed to have any weapons.

ABII Notice

"Due to the imposition of martial law in Tehran, ABII has taken the following action:

1. All personal calls to the United States will be limited to 5 minutes in duration for the next 5 days.
2. The September 14, 1978, picnic is postponed. Please ensure contract employees and any TCI people you have invited are notified."[23]

***

Sunday, September 10, 1978

The curfew in Tehran was relaxed by one hour starting tonight and will be enforced between ten at night to five in the morning.

ABII Notice

"With the current unrest in Iran and the recent imposition of martial law, rumors are running rampant. Needless to say, unconfirmed rumors should not be repeated. It is a time for keeping a 'low profile.' The provisions included in the order of martial law should be strictly adhered to, the curfew obeyed.

ABII, naturally, is concerned with its peoples' welfare, but at this time, sees no cause for alarm. We are in continuous contact with the American Embassy, and they concur with this position.

A person with first-hand experience in this sort of thing is the Reverend Pryor from the Community Church, who gave a sermon on Friday, which in part was based on his nearly 20 years of experience in Iran. He first arrived during the land reform of the early 60s and has lived here before under martial law. His attitude toward the order of Friday morning is to welcome it as a positive step toward easing the present situation, and that in all likelihood, it will produce a calming effect throughout the populace.

To provide as much reliable information as possible to ABII employees, we have set up an information telephone line. If you have any questions regarding the situation, call extension 2207 at the Shah Abbas building.

You can be certain that should conditions change, you will be notified through your lines of organization. As for now, it is 'Business as Usual.'"[24]

"The State Department said 'it is obvious that order must be restored' in Iran and noted security forces appear to be 'reacting with restraint' in putting down the latest disorders.

'We see this situation as essentially an internal affair and while we do not belittle the situation, we believe the Iranian Government remains in control of the situation' says spokesman Charles Shapiro. ...

Shapiro said no deaths had been reported as of noon...and, according to reports received from Tehran, the capital appeared calmer than 24 hours earlier."[25]

***

Tuesday, September 12, 1978

Things have quieted down since last week. The martial law general has moved curfew from nine to ten. Both children like school; however, they both have colds. It's the first time they have been sick since we got here. Each morning on my way to work, I pass a tank and a lorry full of soldiers. I never realized how big those tanks are. Both the truck and the tank are parked down by my office building. The area we live in is patrolled by soldiers and a special unit of police. The area is very well protected and for good reason. Not only are we living here, but a block away is the residence of the new prime minister.

<u>ABII Notice</u>

"How should we interpret the martial law order, as it relates to public gatherings of more than two (2) people?

The intent of this provision is to give the military and police the legal authority to disperse crowds that are gathering, to prevent demonstrations. Buses and taxies, as you are well aware, are running. Businesses are operating. More than the 'magic' number can be seen on the streets at just about any time. ABII will continue to operate functions out of 1717 Pahlavi. The only change in our policy being the doors will close at 8 p.m. until further notice. The film schedule for tonight has been postponed until next week due to the time we originally scheduled it.

Farsi classes will continue to be held in people's homes."[26]

"Opposition Majlis deputies…blasted Premier Jafar Sharif-Emami's government for imposition of martial law on major cities and the shooting of demonstrators on Friday.

Speakers for the government blamed the bloodshed on foreign conspirators and called for cooperation with the new cabinet to allow it to remove sources of discontent.

Mohsen Pezeshkpour said the government had broken the law even before obtaining a vote of confidence from the Lower House; Haj Mohammad Hussein Eshaq-Nejad said the imposition of martial law was a mistake and a clear sign of weakness; and Gholam Reza Akhlaqpour said the Martial Law

Act expressly forbade firing into crowds even though all or some of them might be armed. ...

Pezeshkpour said the present cabinet and its predecessors were the components of the same 'government system' responsible for all that had gone wrong.

He said this system deprived the nation of its sovereignty and transgressed on the fundamental rights of the citizens.

'The despotic government, the totalitarian system...deprived the Legislative and the Judiciary of the power of independent action, destroyed freedom and imposed repression' Pezeshkpour said."[27]

***

Thursday, September 14, 1978

The ABII picnic was canceled for today. Tanks and soldiers were still around. I heard one of the wives of an ABII manager took a picture of the tank and was put in jail, so I won't be taking too many pictures of the army. Today, we played tennis with the Griffeses then had them over for a taco dinner and bridge. We ended early so they could get home before curfew.

The Shah is "cleaning house."Many current and past prime ministers have been arrested or have a warrant out for their arrest. I am amazed at the freedom of speech over here. Ministers and mullahs (local religious leaders) are making very harsh statements about the Shah for imposing martial law. Tomorrow, we will just stay around the house. Rumors state there will be a big demonstration commemorating the deaths of those killed seven days ago. Many of our future weekends may be spent keeping a low profile. Our new theme song is "As Time Goes By."

***

Friday, September 15, 1978

We swam, read, and I played tennis with Nora. Also, we had dinner with the Parkers to celebrate their anniversary.

***

Saturday, September 16, 1978

More of the Shah's cabinet ministers have been arrested for corruption and discrimination. Played tennis with Steve Parker tonight.

"The Prime Minister, Jafar Sharif-Emami, will respond to opposition attacks on his government's program and ask for a vote of confidence from the Majlis today.

The Premier is expected to answer the strong charges that have caused uproar in the Majlis during three days of heated debate that was nationally televised and broadcast to the nation.

The charges revolve around the imposition of martial law; the killing of demonstrators that followed the imposition; the wide-scale corruption that has been responsible for many of the people's grievances; and the unabated power that has grown in the Executive Branch at the expense of the constitutional rights of the legislature, judiciary, press and people's basic freedom."[28]

***

Sunday, September 17, 1978

ABII Notice

"Effective September 17, 1978, the curfew in Tehran is from 11:00 p.m. to 4:30a.m.Due to the above announcement, 1717 Pahlavi will be available for use until 9:00 p.m. every evening except Friday."[29]

"The Majlis approved the government's imposition of martial law on Tehran and 11 other cities after a stormy debate…"[30]

"A Strong earthquake hit eastern Iran yesterday with a severe tremor felt in Tehran.

The quake measured 7.0 degrees on the Richter scale, the Tehran University Geophysical Centre said last night.

It occurred at 7:38 p.m. and the epicenter estimated about 600 miles east of Tehran, a spokesman for the Centre said."[31]

***

Monday, September 18, 1978

We had an earthquake near Tabas, and the death toll is up to twelve thousand and climbing. Iran has declared three days of mourning for those who died.

I picked up some additional responsibilities with my job: contracts, military projects, engineering projects (building, switching, transmission, installation, and the satellite program), operational projects (subscriber trouble reports, training, etc.), and a few minor areas. I enjoy all of it, and it keeps me busy. The weather is starting to cool down about one degree each two or three days.

Nora attended a Tehran American Women's Club pizza and ballet.

"Day after day they marched, tens of thousands strong, defiant chanting demonstrators surging through the streets of Tehran, a capital unaccustomed to shouts and echoes of dissent. The subject of their protest was the policies of Iran's supreme ruler, Shah Mohammad Reza Pahlavi. Some carried signs demanding his ouster. Others called for a return of long denied civil and political liberties and the enforcement of Islamic laws. ...The crowd, at times numbering more than 100,000, was a colorful, sometimes incongruous cross section of Iranian society: dissident students in jeans; women shrouded in the black *chador*, the traditional head-to-foot veil; peasants and the merchants; and the most important the bearded, black-robed Muslim mullahs, the religious leaders of the Shi'ite branch of Islam, which commands the allegiance of 93% of Iran's 34.4 million people.

The challenge to his leadership stunned the Shah and outraged his generals, who argued that the demonstrations were surely eroding his authority—and in turn the army's—and must be stopped. ...

Next day the demonstrations began again and this time ended in fatal, fiery riots. Many marchers apparently had not yet heard the martial-law proclamation over Radio Iran or else they chose to defy it. ...After repeated warnings, the soldiers lobbed canisters of tear gas into the crowd, then shot into the air. As the throngs advanced, the troops lowered their guns and fired. At nightfall, after the bodies of the victims had been loaded into army trucks and carried away, the government announced that 86 people, mostly women and children, had died, and 205 others were wounded."[32]

***

Tuesday, September 19, 1978

Played tennis with Steve Parker in the evening.

***

Wednesday, September 20, 1978

Dear Mom and Dad,

I am really getting spoiled. It is eight thirty in the morning, and the kids are up with Zhari, and I am writing letters in bed. She really makes them toe the line. I think we will save our money and buy or do something special in Greece. Our latest plans are leaving on Thursday, September 28, and get on a cruise ship from October 2 to October 6 and then fly back. That way, John saves vacation days for later, and we really didn't want to see Istanbul anyway. I think Greece would be a great place to meet later on. And our trip to Europe, if all goes right, will be March 15 to April 6. That is, if we can get a tour together. We will get a car in Amsterdam and hotels anywhere.

Let's see, what is new here? The Parkers are home. The kids are very pleased. They are glad to be back. We had them and Webster, who John works with, to dinner Saturday night. Friday, we had our "tennis loss" dinner for John Noske and his son. Gordon and John bet the losers would cook dinner and they lost. Noske played with his son, who is on the Oklahoma State tennis team! We spent ninety dollars split

57

between the Griffeses and us: filet mignon, shrimp dip, tequila sunrise, cake, green salad, and potato salad. We do have some steaks left over. John and Gordon did everything; Joan and I just sat there.

Saturday, I went to the National Arts Museum and watched them make things. I never realized all the work involved in making boxes out of different kinds of wood and metal. The Shah's wife has her clothes designed by an artist, then a pattern is made incorporating each thread, and they intertwine gold thread when setting up weavers. Her wardrobe is beautiful. She must have fifty dresses made that way. I have never seen her in the same dress twice. Then we watched them paint, and they use special English watercolors and cat hairbrushes. Then a weaver let me do a stitch on his rug, and we watched them making the inlaid tables. But those boxes! All those tiny different colors are different pieces of copper, bone, and wood. It really was fun. I will go back again. Everyone was very nice to us, but only three of us went.

I think Americans are afraid to do these sorts of things right now. They canceled all the minibus trips for this three-day weekend and asked us not to go out to dinner or a movie. What a great time to have an anniversary! There was something on the front of the Farsi newspaper but nothing new in the English one. I heard a rumor a movie house was bombed in Mashhad and three hundred were dead or injured, but I also heard the Shah was murdered two months ago. Everything is blamed on communist subversion, and I do believe it is true. These people just are not militant without a strong militant leader. The Muslim Marxists have infiltrated into the church. None of it makes much sense to Westerners who think democracy, free rights, freedom of the press, and women's rights are so important. Enough politics. Iran is a big place, and so is Tehran. We are as removed as Watts was from Arcadia, so don't worry. Today, I will cash a check, see the travel man, and find some of those neat watercolors and some glass for my paintings, so I guess I had better get up.

***

Thursday, September 21, 1978

Played tennis with Gordon, then Nora and I played with the Parkers.

Dear Mom and Dad,

Well, things are getting back to normal. The tanks and lots of the soldiers have disappeared. The Griffeses got a Blazer this weekend, and we set off early Friday morning toward Shemshak. We got off on a dirt road, which was one car wide, and drove straight up a hill full of potholes, dirt, and dust. Joan and Gordon's comment was, "It sure has improved." They had been here before. I guess it washes out each winter. This road is the only entrance to two little villages up in the mountains. The construction is mud huts—no running water and no electricity. We tried to hike up to an Assyrian castle, an old ruin left by the Mongols, but it was too hard with Tori. We ate a picnic lunch, but upon returning to the car, four beers had mysteriously disappeared. We know we had the beer, but we may have put it on the hood when we took the lunch out. I left my purse with one hundred dollars in it, but that was all there, so we really don't know what happened. This road entered the most desolate land I had ever seen—nothing but barren hills. I was really quite glad Joan and Gordon had been on the road before. They say if there is a road in Iran, follow it because it will always go somewhere. Sure enough, after driving awhile, we met some cute kids on horseback from a village. Everyone is very friendly, saying "hello" when we try to speak Farsi. Gordon has crossed the Iranian desert in a Blazer, and Joan set out with three other ladies to visit small villages all over Iran last year. So they really know their way around and are very pleasant to the locals. We gave the kids some candy, took their pictures, and went on. After which, I fell asleep with all the kids. I can't stay awake in the afternoon anymore.

Then today, Joan and I went down to pick up the airline tickets. The traffic was horrid. We left at ten in the morning and got home at two. All we did was cash a check at Shah Abbas, go to the bank, and go to the travel agency; it took that long. On top of all the traffic, they were resurfacing the street. The cars followed the rollers tamping down the new surface, so when you walked across the street, your feet got stuck. After we got the tickets, I was going to take Joan to lunch at the U.S. embassy, so we gave the taxi driver one hundred rials and told him to eat lunch and come back in an hour. He left, and then we found out the embassy was closed. An American couple came up to us. Joan thought I knew them, and she gave Lynn, her eight-year-old who had come with us, to the man and his wife to take her home. As Lynn was driving off in the cab with the couple, I said to Joan, "They seem like a nice couple. How do you know them?" Her answer was, "I thought you knew them." After they left, our taxi came to pick us up. Joan had thought she had heard them call me by name. The taxi driver was very confused, but he is the one who waited at the Hilton beauty shop for me, so he was used to strange things. At the Hilton, I asked the shop clerk for directions. A lady who was getting her eyebrows, toes, fingernails, and hair done came over and spoke to the driver. She was Iranian and very snippy. As an Iranian male, he wouldn't listen to her. It was funny to watch. Anyway, we got home finally (Lynn made it home also).

John and I got ship tickets for a cruise when we go with Joan and Gordon (they weren't interested in cruising). We are very excited as this is the first time we have taken a trip like this. I am taking ballet lessons with Claire, but I don't like it much. All the Iranian workers sit on the roof next door to the studio, eat dinner, and watch us try to dance. It's not much exercise compared to some of the tennis games I am playing. I get free lessons from the club owner! How about that? Thanks for the newspaper clippings.

***

Friday, September 22, 1978

We took a car trip with the Griffeses to visit an Assyrian castle in the foothills. We had a nice picnic. The landscape was barren of any growth except for a few hardy weeds. Other expatriates found this trip worthwhile also but very few Iranians did. We could see the smog floating over the city of Tehran with blue sky above.

***

Saturday, September 23, 1978

The political unrest has eased considerably in Tehran since martial law was imposed. The curfew has been lessened again. It is now from eleven at night to four forty-five in the morning. The tanks and troop carriers have returned to their bases, and the only evidence of martial law is the soldiers with their bayonets. The kids are enjoying school. We are playing tennis two or three times a week. Yesterday, we hiked to an old Assyrian castle outside of Tehran. This coming Wednesday, we leave for Greece for nine days without Tori and John. Nora had ballet tonight. Between that and tennis, she will be in great shape to ski this winter. Nora also started a rug class to learn more about the different tribes and is taking photography and shorthand. She also joined the American Women's Club art guild and plans to have her paintings exhibited at the AWC in December. I am glad she's keeping so busy. Tomorrow is our last televised Monday night football game at one of the ABII buildings, along with beer and popcorn.

***

Sunday, September 24, 1978

Dear Mom and Dad,

Well, I'm sure the first thing on your minds is, "Did we go to a movie in Abadan?" No, we didn't. Everyone is very upset about the killing, and whoever did it doesn't have the nerve to claim responsibility because they would lose their "following." Maybe this will be the end of this type of murder. It isn't aimed at foreigners but Iranians who don't follow Islamic teachings. I still feel it is a communist conspiracy.

I played tennis with Claire on Monday and with Joan today. Joan won but only by 7–5. I usually lose 6–1. The kids are very happy to have the Parkers home. They were gone one afternoon, and John and Tori were driving me bananas. We were going to go to an ABII baseball game, but it was canceled. We and the Parkers spent ninety minutes at Lavizan waiting for a taxi to return and take us home. The game was probably canceled due to the holy period of Ramadan. John brought home a message from the U.S. embassy about maintaining a "low profile" last weekend (Thursday and Friday). We were not to go out to eat, attend a party, play loud music, go to a movie, or go to public places like the bazaar. The tennis club is closed, and ABII buses are canceled. All the Iranian women are covered in black chadors. The maid won't come; she is afraid. The Corricellos went to the Caspian. I envy them but would be rather scared also. ABII canceled all bus trips over the weekend. There are no more tours, movies, and security is checking bags and purses at big hotels and department stores. An armed guard used to be an unusual occurrence but no more. Everything should settle down soon, but they say this is the worst weekend of the year. I read John's book on "writing" and maybe will submit something for the Young Mothers section of Redbook. *What is really ironic is we had a car and so did the Parkers for the weekend. This is unusual. It is the only way we can do something with them since both families need a car; nine in a Peykan is a bit much. The big boring weekend has passed, and there are no newspapers or radio, so I don't know if anything else happened. Last Wednesday, we went to the Evin Hotel with Terry Scott for dinner and snuck in a movie. It was supposed to be for military staying in the hotel. It was a crummy movie but the closest thing to a movie that is available. Saturday, we played tennis and sat up with the Parkers until midnight, drinking Grand Marnier at $4.50 a bottle!*

***

Wednesday, September 27, 1978

We departed for Greece with the Griffeses and left Tori and John with the Parkers. The Parkers would only take John and Tori if they had an official document from the embassy allowing them to take them out of the country if it became necessary. Claire and Nora got that document.

***

Wednesday, October 4, 1978

"The strike at the Telecommunications Company, also for better pay, is today in its sixth day. The managing director of the company, Shamseddin Malek Abhari...presented a scheme to the government for approval. The emergency plan calls for reducing the discrepancy between the highest and the lowest wages from 22-fold to 7-fold to eradicate the enormous difference in salaries.

Bonuses for lower income groups and non-technical staff will also increase. The plan also provides for extra pay for shift workers.

Strikers have not yet responded to the plan."[33]

***

Friday, October 6, 1978

Nora and I returned from our trip to Greece. We left Tehran on September 27 and arrived in Athens around ten in the morning their time. We hiked up the hill that overlooks the Acropolis. It was beautiful and hard to believe the Greeks built it in 400 BC. There was also a sound and light show centering on the Acropolis we went to that first night. Early the next morning, we toured the actual temple before any tourists arrived, walking the very stones the Greeks did way back then. Later on, we experienced the "night life" of Athens. All through the trip, we counted our blessings that we were there after tourist season. There were no people, and the sun was shining every day. We toured the town by bus; they had an excellent bus system. On the twenty-ninth, we did a little shopping and purchased a flokati rug. We then drove to Delphi in a Fiat 127 (each couple had a car). Delphi was beautiful. That night, we stayed just out of town and had the entire place to ourselves. The food and local retsina wine were excellent.

On the thirtieth, we moved on to the small town of Kyllini, and from there, we drove to Olympia while passing through Pyrgos. We all were most impressed with the temple to Zeus. Judging from the size of the columns, the temple must have been huge. At noon, the Griffeses parted company with us. They headed south along Peloponnesus to do the coast route. Nora and I headed east to Athens and then to Piraeus, via Lagkadia, Tripoli, Argos, and Corinth. On the morning of October 2, we boarded a cruise ship for Mykonos. I purchased a gold bracelet for Nora instead of having a porthole on board the ship. The next day, we cruised to Turkey and then Patmos, followed by Rhodes, Crete, Santorini, and then back to Piraeus. Upon returning to Piraeus, the Griffeses met the ship, much to our surprise. We spent the day with them, then flew home. The cruise was great. While on board, we joined another couple from Hawaii who accompanied us during all the island tours. Opting not to take the ship tours, we purchased a book, took buses or rented a car, and conducted our own tours. We enjoyed our new friends as well as the local Greek people. It was all very relaxing. Once back in Iran, we were quickly immersed in martial law, curfew, worker's strikes, the mail strike, and the kids.

Upon landing, which was after curfew, we took a taxi from the airport to our apartments. Near the Shahyad Monument, we encountered a checkpoint. It was pitch dark, but the night was pierced by headlights from several Jeeps, one in front of us and one on each side of the taxi. A soldier waved us down. As he approached the taxi, another soldier stuck his rifle into the car with his finger on the trigger. Several others stood nearby ready to shoot. The taxi driver was talking, as well as Gordon, trying to tell the soldiers we were on our way home from a trip out of the country. Finally, they waved us on. The four of us later joked that if the soldier with the rifle had sneezed, we would all have been killed.

While we were gone, son John was elected to the student council at school. He ran for election all on his own! John starts Cub Scouts this week in his uniform, and both he and Tori start Catholic religion classes next Friday. Tori has started playing "Piruzi school bus."She lines up sixteen chairs in the living/dining room, four abreast, four deep, with a row in the middle. She then puts all her dolls/passengers in the sixteen seats. There are sixteen seats in her actual school bus. We hope to go as a family to Europe in March 1979.

"Strikes for better pay and working conditions have spread across the country, it was reported…

While the Minister of Post, Telegraph, and Telephone, Karim Motamedi announced the proposed increases in pay and overtime for employees at this organization [TCI], the strikes at the Telecommunications Company spread to postal workers. …

A group of workers for the electricity department (Tavanir) in Tarasht, Shahryar, Sari and Farhabad in Tehran have also decided to strike because 'we have not had a pay increase for the last two years,' according to their spokesman. …

Another strike…was at the State Tobacco Monopoly; all production and distribution of tobacco products stopped as employees decided to stop work to demand shorter working hours, more paid holidays and share participation bonuses which at the moment are the privilege of private sector workers. …

At National Iranian Radio and Television (NIRT) headquarters, the employees…prepared a list of their demands which they presented to the political deputy of NIRT, Safaeddin Jahanbani. All workers intend to begin a strike on October 8 if their demands are not met."[34]

***

Saturday, October 7, 1978

This was left on my desk while I was on vacation (the original spelling and grammar have been preserved):

"Dear Employee:

In this political situation, forceful dictatorship of top management of TCI, the budget, the public rights is at the point of explosion. The countries wealth is being robbed by the foreigners.

This company has the environment for nepotism. The predjuice ideas are being used against employees. Those rotten people appear innocent. Instead of the company taking care of these problems logically and stopping this animal behavior, they remained silent. This is unforgivable. This is our national duty to give them notice to perform their responsibility and to take action. After all these years of being taken advantage of, we are to fight for our survival. We will do our best to obtain our human rights which belongs to all Iranians who work honestly to modernize the country.

We give notice that we (regular, contract, partime, etc.) will be on strike on Saturday7 October 1978, by reporting to work but not performing our duties. To obtain our needs which any society has to have. We are not going to listen to the lies and promises of top management.

1. 50% salary raise
2. 50% additional benefits
3. Average of 35,000 rials/month housing allowance
4. Investigate financial dealings of messrs. Malek Abhari, Farkhondar, Firouzabadi
5. Cancel the mandatory contracts made with the Americans

6. Report of progress of American companies and the disposition of the millions of dollars taken from the treasury
7. Discharge all high salaries Americans
8. Establish exclusive hospital with modern equipment
9. Discharge corrupt individuals with bad records and replace with innocent and honest workers
10. Discharge the security department and Mr. Riazei the dirty, rotten pig, to clean the nasty and dangerous environment
11. Establish an employee union with a modern constitution
12. Investigate the purchases made in the last five years especially the hundreds of trailer purchased in the U.S.

We are certain that all employees will join together for a victory to gain valuable human rights instead of the dark, ugly, and dirty situation we now have.

(signed) Real Representatives of TCI"

***

Sunday, October 8, 1978

Riots continue throughout Tehran, and strikes are everywhere. None of the normal services (universities, post offices, government offices, or hospitals) are working. Each day, we hear of more demonstrators killed and wounded, but those hurt and sick cannot receive advanced care.

"Strikes and rallies swept to new areas and sectors as security forces…braced themselves to quell and contain the new wave of disturbances in cities not under martial law.

At the same time, the majority of the nation's 200,000 university students vowed to boycott classes until martial law was lifted in Tehran and 11 other cities, political prisoners were released and freedom of assembly was guaranteed. …

Meanwhile despite Prime Minister Jafar Sharif-Emani's assurances to personnel of the National Iranian Radio and Television Company when he visited the organization last Wednesday that the government would meet their work demands, the network's main staff went on strike…

In Tehran, workers at every government hospital have all but ended medical services for the needy. They have demanded an increase in pay and allowances including housing aid by as much as 100 per cent."[35]

***

Monday, October 9, 1978

"Riot police and troops in armored cars today patrolled Tehran and several riot-hit provincial cities. Strikes paralyzed universities, hospitals and government offices for the third day. …

Student demonstrators rioted in support of strikers demanding pay increases and other benefits in widespread walkout.

Strikes spread in government departments, including state-owned hospitals. The work stoppage by hospital staffs threatened an outbreak of disease. Tension mounted between the strikers and thousands of Asian doctors who stayed on the job.

The strikes shut down the operation rooms of government hospitals, and piled up garbage and dirty bandages. Patients were left without food or only sandwiches.

Pregnant women brought in for delivery of babies were turned back by the strikers. …

Everywhere, universities, schools, power plants, factories, government offices, railroad, bus and mail services were disrupted by continuing strikes."[36]

***

Tuesday, October 10, 1978

"Iran has three new prime ministers. …The prime minister in the morning was Ali Amini, 73, making a bid to return to the position he held in the austerity days of the early '60s . …

The prime minister in the afternoon was Ardeshir Zahedi, 50, Iranian Ambassador to the United States, who is currently in Tehran for consultations. ...

The prime minister [in the evening] was General Fereidun Jam, former chief of the Supreme Commander's Staff and ambassador to Spain. ...

Strange enough, the speculators made no reference to the incumbent prime minister [Jafar Sharif-Emami] who was...hard at work putting the finishing touches to the Government's plan to help striking civil servants." [37]

***

Wednesday, October 11, 1978

Today we received a memorandum to all Iran-based employees regarding emergency procedures. The procedures cover: arrest for any reason, any situation requiring assistance, motor vehicle accidents involving death or obvious personal injury, motor vehicle accidents, motor vehicle mechanical failure, and procedures to follow in the event of a "hit and run." I'm not sure why we are getting this guidance now other than the chances of one of these happening has increased.

"Troops and police opened fire into a crowd of chanting antigovernment demonstrators in downtown Tehran, killing at least three and injuring 85 others. ...

Witnesses said police and army troops charged the student demonstrators with batons and fired tear gas at the crowd near Tehran University before unleashing a volley of fire. ...

A strike by government employees, meanwhile, entered the fifth day. Helmeted soldiers carrying submachine guns patrolled the streets of Tehran and other troubled cities."[38]

***

Thursday, October 12, 1978

I am using the company mail to send personal correspondence to

Nora's parents and mine because there is a mail strike. Life continues as it has been: tennis, parties, driving places to see parts of Iran, school, and high school football games. The only time we're aware of any problems is when we see the troop trucks, tanks, and helicopters in a particular area. TCI is re-evaluating ABII's role over here. We expect to see some future force cuts, maybe as high as 25 percent. My boss worked today, Thursday (our Saturday), to decide how to "force" his organization. On the way to play tennis this morning, he mentioned he may put me in the financial part of the Seek Switch Program, which would involve budgeting, something I enjoy. I told him to put me where he feels I would be the most help. All foreign contractors have to tighten up their belts and make the buck stretch a little further. Every day is an exciting new chapter in Iran. The experience is priceless. Due to general strikes, there is no mail going in or out.

It is starting to get cool, similar to California weather. I called the U.S. Air Force tonight and told them to get on the stick and send me a correspondence course so I can stay active in the reserves.

I played tennis with Gordon and later with Nora. We attended a Tehran American School football game.

***

Friday, October 13, 1978

Played tennis with Nora.

***

Saturday, October 14, 1978

Today was a holiday. We drove to Shemshak foothills for a picnic.

***

Sunday, October 15, 1978

Another memorandum was issued requiring employees and/or dependents who are leaving Iran advise the departure clerk at Shah

Abbas. There is an increased effort to make sure ABII knows where every employee and dependent is. I got a haircut today.

***

Monday, October 16, 1978

Watched a football game with Gordon (Baltimore Colts versus the New England Patriots).

"Tough measures by the army, deploying tanks and armored cars at key sectors combined with patrolling armored convoys and reconnoitering helicopters, won the day in the capital...

Tehran was relatively quiet on the day of national mourning called to mark the 40th day since 'Bloody Friday' on September 8, when martial law troops killed 121 in East Tehran.

Except for some hit and run encounters between the army and demonstrators, no serious incidents took place either in the city or at the Behesht Zahra cemetery where thousands gathered for mass prayers for the dead.

But violence erupted in half a dozen provincial towns, leaving at least 16 dead and hundreds injured. ...

The state radio and television confirmed reports of a general strike, indicating that the economic pulse of the nation all but stopped."[39]

***

Tuesday, October 17, 1978

Nora had a carpet class and pizza with the American Women's Club. Polish Cardinal Karol Wojtyla is elected pope and selects the name John Paul II.

***

Wednesday, October 18, 1978

Nora and I played tennis with Joan and Gordon under the lights.

***

Thursday, October 19, 1978

The first cloudy day since we arrived. I played tennis with Nora.

***

Friday, October 20, 1978

Had the Madhoks over for dinner.

Dear Mom and Dad,

Well, it has been a month since you heard from me, and who knows when you will get this letter. Things go on and everything is an experience. Kathy Dyer came down this morning with her cup of cold water because she has been out of heating oil and the suppliers are on strike. We hurried to play tennis. I will go to the commissary tomorrow, as a gas strike for cars is now on. We went to the store and bought hamburger meat, as the customs people are on strike, and we got milk because the dairy is also on strike. Kathy and I went out to lunch after tennis, and I paid the cab driver an extra one hundred rials because we were late. I am now at the Hilton to get a haircut. I hope the taxi returns. I met the lady who owns Super Parmis, and she says they can't get anything else in stock until customs open up. Prices are skyrocketing— the old story of too many people chasing too few products. It is all very interesting; some people are investing in airline tickets, some are stocking up on food, some are holding cash, and some are buying gold. Claire, Kathy, and I just play it by ear.

I am sitting at the hairdresser wondering how my toes and nails look to someone who is having a pedicure. I am also watching all the bleached blondes looking at my bleached hair wondering why it is so light. I wonder myself sometimes; it must be all the gray hair from being here. Why would someone put glue stuff on their eyebrows? It rained last night, and there is snow on the mountains. Skiing should be here soon. I am taking a photography class and really am enjoying it. Claire and I are also taking ballet once a week. I'm also painting with Kathy. I am starting to work next week, two days a week, as an English teacher for the Iranian Army. I play tennis every day, and we are having our big Halloween party this weekend. We invited sixty people, and costumes are a must. It should be fun, and all the kids are going to scare everyone as they come in the door.

Greece was lots of fun. We had a great time. We shopped in Athens, drove to Delphi, Olympus, and Corinth with the Griffeses. We then were on a cruise of the islands for five days. We danced and drank until two in the morning, wore shorts, ate olives, and loved seeing no chadors. Coming home after curfew was a real thrill. The army stopped us up to eight times between the airport and our house. Not only did they have guns and bayonets, but they pointed them at us from a kneeling position outside the cab, with the cab's inside light on, until the guard talking to the cab driver said it was okay to pass. The tanks and troops have moved down south, so things are a little calmer.

It is now just a question of strikes and what is available for us to eat and use. I can really see the people's point in all this. They really haven't benefited that much from Iran's wealth. Most of the money seems to go to foreigners and the very wealthy. Those who work for the government seem to suffer the most. Even knowing this still makes the strikes inconvenient. A two-week mail strike would be front page news in the U.S. Here, it is nothing, maybe a mention on the third page. Rhodesia is big news, as is Nicaragua, and I feel a sort of premonition about this place going the same direction as Nicaragua. The kids are fine and working on a UN play. Little John asked what the big news was. I told him martial law, and he said, "Oh, he took over for the Shah for a while, didn't he? But the Shah is back now, right?" Obviously, nothing much seems to be bothering them. My hair is done. Khoda Hafez.

***

Saturday, October 21, 1978

The mail strike is still on, as well as dairies, meat processors, teachers, some government workers, bank employees, etc. I feel the

Shah is on shaky ground despite the backing of the military. Almost every Iranian is looking forward to "free" parliamentary elections next year. All I see is a slowdown in the industrial development and more concessions to the mullahs. ABII work is proceeding along an uncertain path. We are trying to decide which contracts to put out to tender and which to cancel in anticipation of cutbacks in funds.

As far as the future for ABII employees, I feel those who are here are probably sure of a job at least for a year or a year and a half. If we are asked to leave, a wind down wouldn't occur until probably mid-1980. I have already seen a cutback in the number of people coming over here. I think this combined with a decrease in spending (due to a delay in the satellite program and the cancelation of stored program control) will keep us in business for awhile.

Snow has already started falling in the mountains behind Tehran. The trees are turning and dropping their leaves. As it gets colder, the barefoot demonstrators are demonstrating less. There was a bus bombed in Isfahan. It was Bell Helicopter employees who were very unfriendly to the locals, referred to by some as the "ugly Americans." I have figured it's hard to get mad at an American who always smiles, speaks a little Farsi, and drives carefully. All expats should remember Iran isn't our country, and as long as we are here, their customs should be our customs. This is how our family conducts itself.

There was a big rainstorm in the evening.

***

Sunday, October 22, 1978

"Panic petrol buying that drained Tehran's 200 filling stations dry by Saturday evening continued throughout [the day], causing traffic jams and ruining taxi-driver's business.

Thousands of motorists queued at stations to fill their tanks in reaction to reports the previous afternoon that the Rey tank farm workers had gone on strike. Some drivers even bought petrol in plastic containers after parking their cars at the side of Parkway…"[40]

***

Tuesday, October 24, 1978

This was left on my desk at work today (original spelling and grammar preserved):

"O, Cursed Yonky
Although you know well about Shah,s Monarkism and his general massacre but while all liberal people condemne this executioner. you and your domned president, support him.
This is the reason that all Iranian people hate you.
Down with Imperialism.
Down with Zionism.
Down with Commonism.
Viva Islam."

While it was U.N. Day at school, given the alerts, I took our flag down. It was cloudy all day.

ABII Notice

"All activities at 1717 Pahlavi are cancelled this weekend beginning at 4:00p.m., Wednesday, October 25 through Friday, October 27.Also, all school activities for Tehran American School have been cancelled this weekend."[41]

ABII Security

"During recent weeks, there have been several confrontations between the police and citizens of smaller cities throughout Iran. At these demonstrations, there have been crowds from several hundred to several thousand people. In Tehran, there have been only minor clashes between the police and civilians. Most of these confrontations have taken place near the bazaar area. Most universities throughout Iran are still closed due to demonstrations by the students.

Another area that could possibly have an effect on people could be the strikes that are occurring throughout the country. There have been strikes by many government organizations; a few of these are the Post Telephone and Telegraph, Ministry of Justice, Minister of Mines and Industry, and Customs.

It is recommended that for the protection of our people that they not become involved in discussing the aspects of these strikes regardless of what organization is being talked about. Our people should, at all times, maintain a low profile and be only concerned with fulfilling our job.

As long as the current situation continues throughout the country, it is recommended that ABII people stay away from areas where large crowds are to gather, such as bazaar area or a university area.

The American Embassy has issued the following alert for the weekend of October 26 and 27, 1978: during the upcoming weekend, the American community should observe normal precautionary procedures, limit movement, and avoid crowds. This is a precaution announcement, and we wish to stress that there is no evidence that there will be disorder. Rumors appear to be just that—rumors. DON'T REPEAT RUMORS."[42]

"The Tehran University campus…was turned into a vast political arena with thousands of students, their ranks swollen by masses of school students, mounting marches, shouting anti-state slogans, listening to tapes of sermons of religious leaders and finally ending the huge rally with mass prayers.

Not all students, however, joined the prayers. A faction, carrying leftist placards emblazoned with 'Unity, Struggle, Victory' and 'Hail to political prisoners, the true sons of the people,' and shouting inflammatory slogans, broke off their meeting before the noon prayers.

Scattered student demonstrations were staged throughout the capital…

In central Tehran, hundreds of students marched along Shah Reza Avenue to the university campus.

The large student body split into two factions on campus, each with its own political coloring, one overly religious and the other Marxist."[43]

***

Wednesday, October 25, 1978

It was a warm evening, so the Parkers, Nora, and I decided to head to the roof for a glass of wine and to watch the sunset. We could hear shooting in the distance. Somewhere close, we also heard the grind of tanks moving down the narrow streets. Many neighbors had joined us on their own roofs. Looking at us, they yelled *"Allah Akbar"* or "God is great!" We looked, waved, and returned the yell to them. They waved, smiled, and the evening wore on. As the tanks below us continued to move through the city, we could hear thuds. I had heard the Chieftain tanks purchased from Great Brittan had long barrels/muzzles, longer than the tank itself. So when the tank was going down cramped streets and trying to turn ninety degrees, the barrel got stuck on the corner of the building. The turret would then swing back and forth. The muzzle would hit the building corner until it gave way. This enabled the tank to continue turning the corner and proceed down the street. While I never saw that happen, it did make sense.

ABII Security
"On Monday, October 23, 1978, at approximately 5:00 p.m., several of the Lockheed minibuses departed Doeshen Tappeh Air Base loaded with employees on their way home. As these buses passed Damavand School, a group of teenagers threw rocks at two of the buses, breaking glass and causing injury to two passengers. Only one passenger was injured seriously enough to have stitches taken above his eye. It is not felt that this incident was prearranged or triggered by any organized group to do harm to expatriates."[44]

"A tense atmosphere gripped Tehran University…after members of a religious student faction tore down posters hung round a sports field by rival Leftist students.

Only quick intervention by several on-looking students prevented a clash between the two factions, which were staging simultaneous rallies on the campus.

More than 7000 Leftist students began a 24-hour sit-in on the field…demanding the release of all political prisoners. …

Earlier they hung posters on the netting around the field, including some which said, 'Toilers of Iran unite' and 'Organize the masses.'

Meanwhile, a similar number of students of the rival religious faction marched around the field, shouting anti-State, anti-American, anti-Russian, and anti-Chinese slogans. They also chanted slogans in support of Ayatollah Khomeini.

The students carried banners with pictures of the exiled Ayatollah and other prominent religious leaders and placards calling for the formation of a 'People's Revolutionary Army.'"[45]

"About 1,200 political prisoners were granted permission to leave Iranian jails today in a gesture of conciliation from the shah to students and teachers who staged fiery demonstrations in five cities.

The shah said he would free the 1,126 prisoners to mark his 59th birthday Thursday. Estimates of the number of political detainees in Iranian jail cells range from 1,670 to several thousand."[46]

***

Thursday, October 26, 1978

I saw tanks driving down Koursh-e-Kabir today. The Shah was flexing his muscle.

"In a massive show of force, the army deployed combat helicopters, tanks, armored vehicles and thousands of armed troops to sweep demonstrators from the capital's streets.

About 4000 students managed to gather around Tehran University on Shahreza Avenue, although troops had blocked all roads leading to the university. …

The students were joined by others from the university and the crowd began moving towards Ferdowsi Square when it was turned away by troops manning the university gates.

Halfway to the square, the troops began firing rubber bullets and tear gas to disperse the crowd.

The students fled down nearby streets, blocking them by moving parked cars. Troops gave chase and made a number of arrests, but no casualties were reported.

Soldiers also fired shots into the air and tear-gas to disperse crowds of demonstrating students in other parts of the capital. ....There were reports that some students had stoned troops."[47]

***

Friday, October 27, 1978

October 1978 is twilight time for Iran. The last six months have certainly been the most difficult for the Shah, as he is trying to bring his country so far so fast. The demonstrations and strikes are still continuing; although, the mail strike has ended after fifteen days. Last Saturday (October 21), we had our first rain since the day we got here. There is already enough snow at Dizin to ski on, but the lifts don't start operations until the end of November. October 24 was UN Day at school. The whole school dressed up in costumes representing the many diverse nationalities. It was an inspiring sight to see children take time to learn the Iranian national anthem and songs from other countries. I didn't even know there was a UN Day; it is supposedly celebrated worldwide. The Shah's birthday was Thursday; he is fifty-nine. We planned our Halloween party for Thursday night, costumes and all, but had second thoughts when the embassy issued a security alert expecting big demonstrations due to his birthday.

After much thought, we decided to have the party anyway. Steve and I had to go to the police station and martial law office to get a permit so forty people could meet in one place. The police and army were very polite in issuing the permit since they thought the party was to celebrate the Shah's birthday. We didn't confuse them with the truth. On the way back to our apartment, we were passed by a tank, five armored cars, a dozen troop carriers, and a couple of Jeeps, all full. They were heading south toward the palace where the Shah was celebrating. I don't know if it was just a show of force or for demonstrations. Our party was a huge success. Not one person canceled due to the alert, and everyone came in costume! As an extra precaution, I tipped the police who watched our street. Today, we recovered from last night and played tennis. I have played more tennis since I got here than I have for the last five years. There is little doubt ABII will be winding down operations here. Future assignments have been canceled. I hope we'll be able to at least finish our tour of two years. The Iranians have a word that describes the lifestyle you have to lead: *Inshallah*, which means "if Allah wills it."

"Scattered violence erupted in Iran for the 11thstraight day, and political unrest appeared to be taking on an increasingly anti-American character. …

More than 1,000 people have died so far this year in the unrest, which has led to imposition of martial law in 12 cities and poses the most serious threat ever to the shah's rule. …

The protests have persisted throughout the country for the past fortnight. They have followed the pattern set earlier this year: mobs storming banks and government offices and burning down theaters and liquor stores. …

The U.S. Embassy here has warned Americans to stay off the streets. There are about 40,000 Americans in Iran, most of who work closely with the military. They are beginning to feel the pressure."[48]

***

Saturday, October 28, 1978

ABII Security

"During the past few weeks, several of our employees have expressed an interest concerning evacuation from Iran should a national crisis occur. There is no indication that the current situation will deteriorate to this point; however, attached is a copy of a memorandum on file at the United States Embassy [no attachment included]. In the event an evacuation was called for by the U.S. Ambassador, the embassy security office would notify ABII security personnel with details. If such a notification is received, we would use our organizational calling method to alert all employees on procedures to follow.

During the past weekend, the situation in Iran was not as critical as many people predicted. In Tehran, it was quiet with only a few confrontations between the police and university students on Shah Reza Avenue. In this area, the police used tear gas to disperse the crowd. There were no reports of injuries. On Thursday, in the town of Jahrom, a sniper killed the police chief and wounded the martial law administrator. In the city of Khorramabad, one policeman was killed during the demonstrations. On Friday, the police in Khorramabad refused to leave the police station because they did not feel they had sufficient backing to confront the crowds.

All ABII employees and dependents are reminded that information distributed by the security organization is not based on our opinion. Prior to releasing information, a check is made with several other American companies' security organizations, the U.S. Embassy security organization, SAVAK, and other contacts that may be appropriate.

For the present, it appears that business can continue as usual. The only suggestion at this time would be for all foreigners to avoid areas where large crowds normally gather, such as the university and bazaar areas."[49]

ABII Security

"At approximately 5 p.m., there were a number of Lockheed and Armish MAAG [Military Assistance Advisory Group] buses leaving the Doeshen Tappeh Air Base. As the buses stopped for a traffic signal near Damavand School, three of the Armish MAAG buses were stoned. The stones broke the windows in all three buses. There were a few people scratched by the glass; however, no injuries were serious enough to require stitches. As you will recall, this is the same location where students threw rocks at the Lockheed minibuses on October 23, 1978. The police have assured American officials that the area will have sufficient police coverage in the future.

There were demonstrations all over the city of Tehran…from Tajrish to the bazaar in south Tehran. The demonstrators numbered from a few to several thousand. …

Employees and dependents are reminded that they should continue to maintain a low profile during the time of social unrest. This includes avoiding the traditional places where large crowds gather."[50]

"Tear gas thickens the Tehran skyline as students join hands in demonstrations that brought traffic to a halt and engaged troops in serious clashes. …

Nineteen students suffered injuries in the most defiant confrontation with security forces since the imposition of martial law in Tehran on September 8th.

The students, numbering several thousand, erected street barricades which snarled dense traffic in central Shahreza and Shah Avenues and impeded the movement of army convoys. Hundreds of motorists were caught in the tie-up and tear gassed.

Police and troops blocked the area around Tehran University and prevented student marchers from approaching the gates of the university which remained shut. …

The entire capital was plagued by demonstrations and sporadic clashes broke out between students and troops and police in east Tehran as well as Kasrodasht in west Tehran, Boulevard Elizabeth, Valiahd (Crown Prince) Square and Shahreza and Shah Avenues. …

The army deployed light Scorpion tanks, armored personnel carriers and machine-gun mounted jeeps in the university area, occupying the entire northern strip of Shahreza. At one time, Tehran's main thoroughfare was closed to vehicular traffic."[51]

"At its best, this city is a terrible for town traffic.

With an estimated 1.2 million vehicles in a city of 5 million, traffic on the broad avenues is choked most of the time on any working day.

The current wave of unrest and demonstration has made it that much worse, and Saturday it could only be described as true chaos. It was the start of a student protest week, and thousands of young people joined the usual traffic in clogging the streets.

By and large, the students were on their best behavior. At least several of the groups marching toward Tehran University kept together in the midst of traffic, and stopped and waited patiently along with the cars for the traffic lights to change. …

Generally, there were enough soldiers on hand on the main streets to keep the traffic moving, though slowly, and they were backed up by fire department water cannon which were used to encourage the students to move rapidly. There were a few tense moments near Tehran University, and tear gas grenades were used several times."[52]

***

Sunday, October 29, 1978

"Swirling riots left a trail of destruction across downtown Tehran…rampaging students adopted hit-and-run tactics against security forces.

The Europa cinema and two liquor shops were burned on Shahabad Avenue, five beer delivery trucks were attacked by youths shouting anti-government slogans, and bank windows were smashed. Most shops closed early for fear of looting.

Squads of the estimated 100,000 troops patrolling the downtown area moved in to disperse the youths, most of whom were teenagers or adolescents, but there were no reports of casualties.

At about noon the troops ended their lock-out of Tehran University, and as the campus gates swung open, thousands of students poured in.

A giant rally was staged on the campus by about 6000 students chanting religious slogans. …

Outside the university, groups of students gathered suddenly at intersections, shouted anti-government slogans and then raced off to regroup somewhere else. These hit-and-run tactics kept troops on the move and prevented bloody clashes. …

Military units were reinforced around Shahyad Square as rumors spread that thousands of demonstrators were planning to destroy the multi-million-dollar monument built in 1972. Tanks and truck-mounted machine guns were deployed around the square, but the march failed to materialize.

Elsewhere, however, troops fired tear gas to disperse groups of demonstrators who gathered at numerous intersections in the busiest part of the city.

Traffic jams mounted and many drivers found themselves inadvertently caught in clouds of the stinging gas."[53]

***

Monday, October 30, 1978

"At Tehran University 20,000 students gathered from early morning at the sports field and shouted various slogans, some urging the unity of students and professors.

Precautionary steps were taken at the university, with only the south gates open, when rumors spread that groups wielding sticks would enter the university and start attacking students.

Checks on the student identification cards are no longer made because many students from different institutions of higher education and schools enter the campus to join demonstrations.

Security forces…did not interfere with the demonstration, but guards were ready in case the rumored attack took place."[54]

***

Tuesday, October 31, 1978

Dear Mom and Dad,

Hi. Well, we have been very busy. We had our Halloween party. Claire and I called Auto Charlie, and they wrote us a note in Farsi saying we were having twenty-five people until ten thirty. Then Claire and I took it to the police station past the armed guards only to be told, "Your husbands have to settle such matters." So the next day, John and Steve went up to the station, got frisked, and got permission to have the party. Well, we had forty people until 11:45p.m. Everyone came in neat costumes. We had the Scarecrow, the Pink Panther, cats, pillowcases, and even "Ralph and Alice" (code words for the Shah and the Shabanu). The kids judged the costumes and "scared" people as they came in. Everyone ate all the ham and turkey, but only twelve rolls (unusual). We finished all the food and drinks and decided it was about seventy dollars apiece (for the Parkers and the Doolittles each). It was really fun, and people were so ready for a good time. Renee had a party for the kids Halloween night, and they sat and listened to The Hobbit with their popcorn balls and five treats and thought it was wonderful. At home, they would never be satisfied trick-or-treating at six houses, but here, it was super. John had his sword made from his Piruzi flag stick

83

and a cottage cheese tin, a black cloak, and my white hat with black material. Leslie had on her mom's leotard, and Kathryn was a cute pumpkin. There were fourteen kids in all, and they all had fun.

Renee was caught in a demonstration in Mashhad in a chador and had to ride eighteen hours on a bus with the Shiite pilgrims. What a story! The chador saved her life probably. I refuse to wear anything. It is against my principles! Women's lib over here means going out without your hair covered!

Everyone thought I was crazy, but I took the job at the Army Staff Command College as an English teacher, and I love it. The first day, no one was leaving their houses, school was out, demonstrations were supposedly everywhere, and I had heard we were picked up in an army Jeep and went near Tehran University. I must admit, I was nervous, but they picked us up in a station wagon with an army man in plain clothes. We saw no demonstrations, and it was super fun. I work from nine thirty to one thirty. I have two two-hour classes of sixteen majors each. They all speak English fluently, so it is a real challenge to figure out what to teach. It is basically conversation, expressions, and grammar. They ask the funniest questions and really throw you. Today: "What does dizzy mean?"; the difference between static on a radio and fluctuation; the difference between "for sale" and "on sale"! All these things one never thinks of. Anyway, it's fun, and what is wrong with the sentence "I want a good cheaper one"? Why is that wrong? I had to think on that one. Is it "I want a good cheap one"? The girls I work with are really nice, and I've lasted two days so far, and we have talked about Bay Area Rapid Transit (BART), cars, me, buying in the US, and catalytic converters. Thank God I have husband John's high school English book. "What is the difference between on time, in time, and at eight o'clock? Why do we go to a restaurant for dinner but eat in a cafeteria?" I'm glad I am not trying to learn English. It's hard enough to know it and try to explain it. Anyway, with all the turmoil going on, I am concerned with the past participle of the verb "to be." One last incident, which was interesting. When I walked into the class the first time, the students asked me what my husband did. I said he worked for Bell Telephone, but before I could get the word "telephone" out, they started to stand up and leave. Some of my better students explained it was the "telephone company," not "Bell Helicopter." In Iran, a woman represents what her husband does, and apparently, these officers were not fond of Bell Helicopter. I had *another student who said he was going on a trip to "Frisco." I gasped and said, "What?" He said Frisco again, and I said, "No, no. No one ever goes to Frisco but only 'The City' or 'San Francisco.'" He asked why: "You go to LA and the Big Apple, why not Frisco?" I told him "The City" or "San Francisco" period. He finally said, "I am going to San Francisco."*

John is fine, and so are the kids. Schools are open, we have cooking fuel again, and no problems in our neighborhood. I still haven't seen any anti-Americanism. Everyone I see is very nice and friendly. I don't have a maid and am working so it cuts into the time. Zhari came back one week late. I felt terrible, but I let her go as I had found someone else, but then she turned out to be a dud, so I want Zhari back.

***

Wednesday, November 1, 1978

Demonstrations have been going on since September 8, when martial law was declared. They have only turned serious during the last few days, though. A fire started today, and windows were broken at the Iran Telecommunication Company Kakh Street building. Some cars were burned in front of the building. The Iran TCI employees walked out at one thirty due to a bomb threat and did not return. The ABII employees remained until later in the afternoon. Today was the fourth day of student demonstrations, the largest at Tehran University. Shops closed near the university, and the owners and employees joined the demonstrators. Eventually, the demonstration dispersed. There was no school today.

ABII Security

"During the past few days, we have continued to see demonstrations here in Tehran; however, we are now experiencing demonstrations in the northern part of the city…there were demonstrations at a small university just off Saltanatabad—also on Niavaran, Tajrish, and numerous other locations throughout the city.

During the evening of November 1, 1978, there were two vehicles burned near Farmanieh and Saltanatabad. Both unattended vehicles were equipped with service license plates, which are issued to individuals with diplomatic status. One vehicle belongs to a lieutenant colonel in the U.S. Air Force; the other vehicle is owned by an attaché from the Australian Embassy.

On November 1,1978, at approximately 4:45p.m., there was a fire on the first floor of the Kakh Street Building. The area of the fire was a room TCI uses for storage of records and other combustible materials. The damage to the building appears to be about $140,000. There is no reason at this time to suspect arson as the cause of this fire.

During the past week, several people have called, asking if they were registered with the U.S. Consulate. Each employee fills out an embassy card at the time that they make application for a residence permit. The card lists all dependents that are in Iran. Each employee should be reminded that should an evacuation be called for by the U.S. Ambassador, ABII will be notified by the embassy with the details of the evacuation. Upon receiving the notice from the embassy, ABII would use the organizational calling method to alert employees and dependents. Again, there is no indication that an evacuation will be forthcoming. The information above is given to clarify questions from employees and dependents."[55]

"In Tehran...tens of thousands of persons paraded in the streets to express their joy over the release of holy man (Ayatollah) Taleghani. Minor incidents were reported. At Tehran University, 20,000 students gathered peacefully on the campus to shout anti-government slogans and mix with opposition political leaders. ...
Troops sealed off the streets leading to the Iran Telecommunication Company building on fire at Kakh Avenue."[56]

***

Thursday, November 2, 1978

Nora played tennis. There was a going away party for several employees today, but we did not attend. We played bridge with the Griffeses instead.

"Security forces battled about 2,000 students outside of Tehran University in one of the worst clashes in the capital since martial law was imposed September 8.

According to reports the rampaging students attacked a cinema theatre in the vicinity of the university campus as well as several restaurants and banks.

Though security forces had to use batons and tear gas to break up the demonstration, no serious injuries or arrests were reported.

During the demonstration students reportedly passed out pamphlets to bystanders, issued by a group calling itself the 'Party of God,' giving instructions on how to make 'Molotov cocktails' and calling on the public to arm themselves."[57]

***

Friday, November 3, 1978

We attended the Tehran American School football game with the Parkers and Papas. Finished off the evening with a glass of brandy.

"Former US Secretary of State Henry Kissinger said today that the Carter Administration's emphasis on human rights has helped cause turmoil in Iran and may jeopardize prospects for peace in the Middle East.

Kissinger, speaking to a gathering of the World Jewish Congress, noted that a pro-Western, stable Iran is absolutely essential for a stable Middle East.

'The Shahanshah of Iran is caught between those who think he is moving too fast (to modernize Iran) and those who think he is moving not fast enough,' Kissinger said. 'Abstract human rights slogans by the United States are accelerating this process.'

On Thursday, ABC News reported that the Carter Administration has warned the Iranian regime against a tough crackdown against workers who are striking against Iran's oil operations, and that Carter is afraid of losing the support of human rights advocates in the United States.

'If the Iranian regime is replaced with a more radical one,' Kissinger warned, 'the prospects for peace, which make us all so hopeful today, will be dramatically altered.'

The fall of Iran, he said, could lead to a total radicalization of the Middle East, which would make American concern over the validity of some regimes relatively trivial.

In Washington, Henry Precht, head of the Iranian desk in the U.S. State Department, said in a broadcast interview last night that we are 'deeply disturbed about the current political developments in Iran. The situation in the country is quite serious at the moment.'…

Asked if the Shahanshah might step aside, he [Precht] answered 'no.'

He was asked what might happen if the situation deteriorates further to which he answered one possibility is that the military will take over.

Precht said the 40,000 Americans living in Iran were not in danger.

Meanwhile, US Secretary of State Cyrus Vance praised the Shahanshah as a 'very close and valued ally' and issued a strong appeal for an end to the upheavals which have shaken the Monarchy. …

Vance said he hoped the Monarch would continue with his plan for economic and political reform despite the continuing violence and strikes.

Following a Pentagon statement that there were no plans to evacuate any of the estimated 41,000 Americans who live and work in Iran, a spokesman for Bell Helicopter-Textron Company, Tim Gette, said the company had no plans to pull out its 3,500 employees in Iran.

'Our general policy is to follow the directions of the US embassy and the US military. We operate at their direction, so we would do whatever they decide,' Gette said.

Ed McCurdy, director of the Parsons Construction Company…said his company was preparing plans for an immediate evacuation of its 45 employees in Iran, if it was deemed necessary."[58]

"Religious leader Ayatollah Khomeini said here today he had 'not yet given any assent to unleash civil war' but that he might change his mind.

In an interview with a French radio station, he also called for an end to the present regime. ...

Khomeini warned that if other countries continued to back the regime, civil war would break out. But if they dropped their support, a 'quick solution to the problem' could be found.

Khomeini said he wanted to see an Islamic republic set up after a referendum vote and restoration of 'total independence.'..."[59]

***

Saturday, November 4, 1978

The U.S. embassy is stepping up security measures. Fires broke out in downtown Tehran, windows were smashed, and some cars were burned. While no major corporations have left Iran, some of the smaller ones have. We were advised that "care" should be exercised when traveling to the provinces. ABII is increasing building security measures. Today, there was a bomb threat at the Kakh Street building and at TCI-2. At the Seek Switch building, demonstrators surrounded the perimeter while employees locked themselves inside. No one was able to leave until after eight at night. A few of the cars parked in front were burned too. If an evacuation was necessary, we would adhere to the U.S. embassy evacuation plan.

ABII Notice

"As you know, the Iran Gas Company is on strike and will be for an indefinite period. As a result, Normal Distribution outlets have been closed. In our effort to find a place where we could get gas, we found that if you bring your empties to the Iran Gas Company at 110 Lahijani St., you should be able to get replacements. We don't know how long the supplies will last, so act quickly. Good Luck."[60]

"Mobs ran wild through most of west and central Tehran...on a destructive rampage that was touched off by troops opening fire outside Tehran University causing several casualties.

Bloody rioting exploded until well after dark spreading from outside the university campus on Shahreza Avenue, north towards Kakh and Aryamehr Avenues and south to Shah, Maiden Youssefabad, Hassanabad and Lalehzar.

The firing at the university gates left a confirmed toll of at least three deaths and 30 injured. But there were widely conflicting reports...

The martial law administration denied there were any deaths in the firing ...But the students reported that there were 65 deaths while radio and television news said four people had been killed and the toll was thought to be much higher. ...

The rioting was triggered off outside the main gates of the university on Shahreza. Students spilled out of the campus after peaceful rallies during the morning and began to march to the home of religious leader Ayatollah Teleghani who was released from detention last week.

They were confronted by security forces outside who asked them to disperse in small groups and not block the heavy traffic on Shahreza with a huge procession.

When they refused to disperse, troops first used water cannon, hurled tear-gas and then fired into the air. But it failed to stop the students. ...

The troops, who were under heavy attack, were forced to run for cover and then open fire with automatic weapons to stop the students when they began burning vehicles in the roadway to set up barricades between themselves and the security forces.

It was only the first volleys of gunfire that dispersed the students with many regrouping behind the university gates and high fence to continue pelting the troops.

Several students were seen hit by the gunfire and a number of them were carried back wounded onto the campus.

The firing, which took place shortly after noon, was then followed by rampaging mobs taking to the streets carrying banners and shouting slogans '65 were killed in front of the university.'"61

"Troops opened fire on 6,000 students who tried to demolish a statue of the Shah, killing five people and injuring several others in the bloodiest riot in Tehran in two months.

A series of politically motivated strikes spread to gasoline stations and the telecommunications company, but Iran's oil industry, nearly paralyzed by a walkout, reportedly was back up to a third of its normal daily output.

The strikes and anti-government street demonstrations have put Iran under the greatest open pressure since Shah Mohammad Reza Pahlavi came to power 37 years ago.

Witnesses said thousands of students who gathered at Tehran University for an anti-shah protest went on a rampage through the downtown area, attacking banks, shops and government buildings and setting fire to at least six cars. …

The five deaths and several injuries reported by Iranian television was the highest death toll in a Tehran riot since the 'Bloody Friday' massacre by Iranian troops Sept. 8 that killed and injured hundreds of people.

Security units had to use teargas grenades to disperse another group of anti-government demonstrators in an area near the university that is the site of many government offices."[62]

***

Sunday, November 5, 1978

Fires in Tehran. No gas stations open. Curfew was moved back to 9:00 p.m.–5:00 a.m.

There was another bomb scare at Kakh Street and the TCI building. The TCI employees did not go to work since they were on strike. We heard that fifty thousand demonstrators were on their way up Koursh-e-Kabir (where the ABII building was), so at one thirty, we sent ourselves home. Multiple fires erupted in downtown Tehran. Expatriates are now in a difficult position. The revenues associated with the various projects over here are, in most cases, low compared to the capital invested, so the Iranians are not seeing much return for their money invested at this time. While there is some talk about evacuation, President Carter and the Shah cannot politically afford to openly discuss any plans that would

91

result in the U.S. leaving. The attitude of all ABII employees is "business as usual."Some of the Iranians I work with are saying ABII will not be around after November 21.

As I looked out the window this afternoon, I saw troops and tanks moving north up Koursh-e-Kabir from downtown. At six o'clock, Jim Wade passed on an embassy alert telling us not to go to work tomorrow. That translated to "no school" also. We will be called when it's time for us to return. There could be possible utility strikes, so we are to stock up on water, food, and flashlight batteries. The ABII rumor is we will be home by Thanksgiving. At home, while listening to the six thirty news on television, I learned many students were killed on the fourth. Today, the army left the students alone, so crowds attacked and destroyed buildings on Kakh Street, north along Pahlavi Boulevard. Whole blocks were gutted with the exception of a few small shops, and troops did nothing to restrain demonstrators. Banks, hotels, and cars were burned. The Shah's Prime Minister, Jafar Sharif-Emami, might resign tomorrow. Oil refinery employees, other than those in Abadan, went on strike today. The army is taking over the oil refineries.TCI employees are threatening to cut phone lines to the outside world if political demands are not met (i.e., 1. all political prisoners freed, 2. no martial law, 3. no repercussions from SAVAK [Shah's secret service]). They will also destroy microwave towers in various locations. At seven in the evening, we found out there is no school tomorrow, and at nine thirty the American Women's Club called advising all Americans to stay off the streets tomorrow. Nora and I watched a *Hopalong Cassidy* western at ten o'clock then went to bed.

"Small groups of people rampaged through the streets of the capital attacking and setting fire to banks, cinemas, government buildings, liquor stores, hotels, and vehicles while troops looked on passively. Only strategic buildings, including the American Embassy, were heavily protected. ...

The unprotected British Embassy on Ferdowsi Avenue was also attacked in the evening.

The damage caused during the day is estimated at around $500 million dollars."[63]

"The Prime Minister of Iran resigned tonight after demonstrators demanding the ouster of Shah Mohammad Reza Pahlavi rampaged through the streets of Tehran setting fire to buildings. Strikes spread through the country, further crippling oil production and other industries.

The Shah, who is fighting an increasing challenge to his reign of 37 years, turned to the armed forces to help restore order, and the authorities announced that they would strictly enforce martial law, which was imposed in 12 cities in September, and shoot rioters and strikers in vital industries. …

The wave of demonstrations, which have engulfed Iran for the last 10 months, has left more than a thousand dead. The demonstrations have been aimed at putting pressure on the Shah to enforce Islamic laws and halt his moves toward modernizing this traditionally Islamic nation, release all political prisoners, crack down on corruption and end martial law.

The rampages today in Tehran, in which the British Embassy and dozens of banks, office buildings and movie theaters were set on fire, followed the shooting of university students by troops during clashes…At least three persons were killed…when soldiers fired through, the gates of Tehran University at jeering, rock-throwing students. …

After the rioting, a curfew that has been in effect during the last six weeks was moved up to begin at 9 p.m. instead of midnight."[64]

***

Monday, November 6, 1978

There were no buses to work; Americans were advised to stay home. No school. The British embassy was damaged yesterday; however, the American embassy was protected by the Iranian Army. Hotels were also burned. Martial law is in effect, so no gatherings of more than two people. If groups do not disperse when warned, they will be fired upon. Liquor stores were broken into, and the liquor was used to start fires in various shops. Large groups of people rampaged through Tehran yesterday, burning cars and buses.

Prime Minister Jafar Sharif-Emami resigned, and a new prime minister was assigned: General Gholam Reza Azhari. Sharif-Emami lasted seventy-one days. This puts in place a military government to help prepare the country for free elections.

Almost all major business buildings have been victims of bomb threats. My parents called this morning. They were worried about the situation over here and told us Bechtel employees were packing up and leaving. I reassured them and told them we would call Nora's parents Friday. At four fifty Webster called. The embassy had stepped up security measures and had gone to "red alert." I was told the Eighty-Second Airborne in Germany had been put on alert, but none of us are sure what that means. I think there are forty-one thousand Americans in Iran, so the logistics of getting all of us out would be monumental. There were fires in south Tehran all night, and this morning, lines had formed of people trying to get food. Demonstrators are using Molotov cocktails now. There is no work or school tomorrow.

A strike has closed down the *Kayhan International* newspaper, our main source of news.

A few small corporations have packed up and gone home, but the big ones are still here: Bell Helicopter, ABII, and Lockheed. Security at ABII has been brushing up on the embassy evacuation plan, but I think we are still a long way from that. ABII employees at the Seek Switch building were prevented from leaving by demonstrators. They finally got out with police support at nine at night. None of these demonstrations "have it in" for the Americans at this point. The reason employees couldn't get out of the building(s) was because of the massive crowds outside.

We photographed all our furniture and possessions that may get left behind if we pull out. There are still huge lines of people to get food.

Dear Mom and Dad,

Well, it's the day before the elections in California, and I wish Sunne McPeak luck (she is running in a local election). What a difference— women running for public office and going out of your house without a "damn chador." John is home; school is canceled until Sunday. Sharif-Emani's government is gone. There is no word from the Shah. People are packing. The fires are up to Takht-e-Jamshid and Shah Abbas streets, and everything is very quiet in the provinces. So it is an organized march in Tehran. The kids are so normal. John woke up at eleven thirty this morning with an ear infection, and thank God we had some penicillin from Tori's ear infection last weekend. Tori is busy cutting out letters and gluing them on paper. The smartest thing I have done here is save all the packing paper for drawing. She sits for hours drawing, cutting, and pasting. John is working on a poster for school for "good manners week." He is so proud of being on the student council. John and Steve Parker just walked to the store for meat, candles, penicillin, milk, and eggs. There was a "run" on food last night. Joan (Griffes) waited half an hour to get into her koochek store, but all seems very peaceful here. The kids will be home for five days. I don't know about my teaching job. I think they should cancel it.

I don't know when John will go back to work. A lot of ABII buildings are burned and the windows broken. John's Iranian counterparts are on strike. They threw things at ABII employees at the Kakh Street building as they left. John heard at twelve thirty that there was a bomb threat at his building at eleven. Cute, but no bomb. John and Peggy [John's parents] called last night, so who knows what the papers are saying in the U.S. I imagine it is coming across like Nicaragua, but I don't know what the outcome will be here. I think the army is stepping up action. I can't imagine the officers sitting through an English class tomorrow. Rumor has it to stock up on food, water, and candles and that the phones will be out by Wednesday. We are not scared or frightened, and I think the worst situation would be to leave with the first Americans out. I am sure they will be the panicked and obnoxious ones. Large crowds of frightened, scared people scare me more than troops, fires, and bombs. The news says the British Embassy was attacked, and troops stopped an attack on the U.S. embassy. I wanted to go there for lunch and shopping today. We still have not had anything directed at us, and all the Iranians we have met are friendly, courteous, and nice. I still say it is a communist conspiracy. I am not going to write to the Bairds anymore. Every time we write, we comment on something that hasn't happened yet, and when they get the letter, it has happened! The news says we have a general for the prime minister.

I walked down to Kathy Dyer's to give her some milk, and they are packing. She is unstuffing her pillows, and I'm using her stuffing for mine. We discussed going to Andorra to live for awhile. Being "low profile" can be such a bore. The kids have all the chairs in the house

95

lined up like a bus, and they are playing "Piruzi Bus." Now we have a cabinet made up entirely of generals. Tonight, the Parkers came up, and we had some drinks and talked about everything.

"The Ayatollah Ruhollah Khomeini, the Moslem leader who heads the Iranian opposition movement from exile, called on the Iranian armed forces to turn against the shah and 'join the people' against 'the traitor.'"[65]

***

Tuesday, November 7, 1978

It's calm today, business as usual. Looks like the military government is working. We didn't go to work again today, and there is no school until November 12.

Dear Mom and Dad,
The house is freezing. We had no heat last night. John is home again today (no work), and school for me was canceled. He is trying to fix the heater, and he looks like a chimney sweep. The kids are driving me bananas. I will go to work tomorrow. John just fixed the heater! He filled the tank with water on the roof. How he figured that out I'll never know.

We are out of bread. Claire said she would make some if I gave her flour. I wonder if the taxicabs are working today. Steve said there were five hundred people up at the gas station last night. Steve and Gordon went to work today, as they are district level or third level managers (John is second level). I think things will be quiet for awhile. I am supposed to have a friend of Zhari's coming as a house cleaner two days a week. She is an old woman with no teeth. John will walk down and see if there is a paper. There wasn't one yesterday (and there wasn't one today). A friend of mine's husband works for Oman Bank, and they have lost twenty branches. I have a funny feeling Sunne lost the election. I hope I am wrong. As soon as the dryer is done, we will plug the coffee pot in the transformer and then listen to the news. We only have one large transformer. There was no national news until three, and then we heard all was quiet except for the burning of an eleven-story building.

How sad, their computers and all records were destroyed, and some died. Claire and I walked to the koochek market, and it really reassured us. No Iranians said anything derogatory, and the man who worked there even went upstairs and got me a dozen eggs and some milk he had saved for our children. Rumor has it places aren't selling food to Americans—not true here. John goes back to work tomorrow, and I don't teach until next Tuesday. We had ten kids in and out today; they played Risk, and I baked a cake and meatloaf with five eggs! All is very normal now. We are warm, dinner is cooking, and the kids are at the Parkers. Kathy is calmer now, and even Ken doesn't have any new rumors. The news tonight was just a voice on TV saying the military government has arrested a number of people. It was like 1984 or Big Brother. They mean business.

"Shah Mohammad Reza Pahlavi's two-day-old military government, trying to quell violent opposition to the monarch's authoritarian rule, announced the arrest...of at least 35 former ministers and ranking civil officials. ...

The government warned that persons violating martial law regulations would be dealt with severely. Forty tanks were moved into the capital from garrisons on the outskirts of the city to bolster armor already on guard at key points.

Many banks remained closed, as well as shops in and near the bazaar, which had been the starting point for much of the unrest in recent weeks. Scores of banks branches were destroyed by rioters Sunday and their records scattered or burned. ...

Scattered violence erupted in downtown Tehran...but there were no serious clashes as demonstrators fled before troops arrived. Small groups of anti-government demonstrators tried to approach Tehran University as troops closed off streets leading to the campus, but they dispersed as troops fired into the air. Witnesses said several youths were beaten by club-wielding police."[66]

***

97

Wednesday, November 8, 1978

Today was a "nothing day."Ever since the new cabinet was appointed, there have been no newspapers or local news on the radio or television. So much for freedom of the press! I did not work on the sixth or the seventh, and the kids are not scheduled to go back to school until the twelfth (Nora is ready to climb a tree). The Iranian telephone employees are still on strike, so they were not at work today. This weekend will be another "low-profile" one. A party scheduled for Thursday night has been postponed, not because of the curfew but because of a gas strike. Most of the gas stations are out of gas, and the ones operating have quite long lines.

Dear Mom and Dad,

John is at work, and so Claire and I are going to Shah Abbas with some kids. Her maid Zahari got me a new maid, but she didn't show up. Shah Abbas was amazing. It was rather a "calm" panic. Rumors ran wild, and there were three lines going down the stairs to cash checks for rials and traveler's checks. They opened at nine in the morning, and by nine thirty, they were out of checks. We waited until 9:45 for rials. We heard Khomeini said on the radio telling Iranians to take up arms now and that they had guns in Qom. People are pulling out. Then we went shopping at Behdask, and things seemed normal, but there was some tension in the air. Our taxi driver coasted as much as possible to save gas as the lines are still very long. After shopping, Claire, Kathy, and I went to the Pars Club for lunch. The "ugly American" was there. The whole place made me very nervous. If one hated foreigners, I can't imagine a better place to bomb than this club. The type of people who sat around and drank when the Titanic sunk were the type of people there now. The Dyers had us back for burritos, a first in six months, and we took all the kids to our house to spend the night—all before nine o'clock.

"The Iranian military put on a show of force...and martial law authorities arrested an ex-prime minister in a campaign to discourage opposition to Shah Mohammad Reza Pahlavi. ...

Troops backed by tanks and armored personnel carriers guarded key areas of the city and its giant bazaar, which was closed. The bazaar, which also contains the huge Shah Mosque, has been the staging area for many of the anti-Shah demonstrations that have erupted since January. …

The imperial palace denied rumors that an attempt had been made on the life of the shah. Rumors circulated in the United States that a shot had been fired at the ruler."[67]

***

Thursday, November 9, 1978

A "low-profile" day. Played tennis with the Craigs, followed by beer and chips at their home.

Dear Mom and Dad,

Today, the Dyers came for breakfast and then took all the kids to the Pars Club while John and I played tennis with Eddie and Ron Craig. We went with the kids to the Craig's' place, which was very nice. They took us in their Mercedes, not too low profile! We didn't get home until five, after talking all afternoon without mentioning rumors and politics. It was fun, and we will see them again for tennis on Saturday. At six thirty, I listened to the news and damn this place; they canceled school until November 18. What the hell do you do with the kids? If they go back on the eighteenth, that is eleven days in November of school…that's it. I am ready to leave. I want to take the kids to England, put them in school, get a little job of some sort, and wait and see what it is like in January. It is too expensive to go home and come back, and John has used up all his vacation. We hear nothing on the news about what is happening. We went downstairs after the kids were asleep and drank with the Parkers. I am gaining weight!

***

Friday, November 10, 1978

Another low-profile day. Played backgammon with the Dyers. The rumor mill is really turning. With no newspapers or local news, people rely on what others hear and pass on. I'm sure, in most cases, this is worse than the truth. We have a call to Nora's parents tonight. Our social life consists of playing tennis and sitting around talking and drinking. One of the hardest items to find now is liquor. Fortunately, my Air Force Reserve status gives me access to the embassy store. We heard yesterday that the kids won't go back to school until the eighteenth. If the schools continue to stay closed, we will need to make some special arrangements. One choice may be to send Nora and the kids to London for two or three months. Some companies have already done this. The rumor today is the Shah told Carter he wanted to abdicate, but Carter told him not to. Tomorrow is supposed to be the day civil war starts in Iran. The next few weeks will tell the tale as far as the Shah is concerned. Fourteen F-4 jets arrived at the Tehran military airport yesterday—maybe a show of strength?

Today, it rained in the morning. I went to church and found out they canceled all Catholic religion classes due to the troubles. So much for religion training for Tori and John.

Dear Mom and Dad,

Today, they canceled religion class at church until after the eighteenth. Why? I don't know. There are new rumors: the Shah called Carter and said he wanted to abdicate, and Carter said no; evacuation has started; fighter planes are here from Germany; and civil war will start this weekend. Here are some "facts": planes leaving Tehran are full; moving companies are out of packing material; there is a two-month backlog to move; the warehouses are full; a cab driver was shot and killed on Saltanatabad Boulevard; there is no more liquor in the stores; and tomorrow is the day they slaughter sheep in the street. The jubes run red with blood.

***

Saturday, November 11, 1978

It is Veterans Day today, a holiday.

8:30 a.m.

It's supposed to be a big day for demonstrations; however, it is raining. That may slow them down. We were going to play tennis with the Griffeses this morning and the Craigs this afternoon (Ron Craig works for General Dynamics). Maybe the courts will dry later this evening. Today is a Holy Day in the Shiite religion. Each Islamic family kills a lamb, roasts it, and eats it. I noticed this morning the family next door was already up and at it; they beheaded the lamb and are now skinning it.

Nora and I stayed up last night and discussed the current situation. Tomorrow, Nora is going to get some traveler's checks and a good supply of rials. London for Nora and the kids is looking to be a good option. She would put the kids in school there and try to get a job. Friends of Nora's parents live there, so at least she would know some people. A lot depends on what happens the next few weeks. There is a small chance that ABII may be asked to leave before the end of the year; cutbacks in money for the program plus resentment from Iranian employees may force TCI to eliminate us. There's also the slim chance of a civil war, in which case we would leave. With no news, it is very difficult to make plans. I heard the English newspaper in Tehran was destroyed. We don't know if it was done by the demonstrators or the military because there is—you guessed it—no news. The TV and radio stations are now under the control of the military, so they are playing nothing.

9:00 a.m.

It is still raining. Nora is working with Tori on learning her alphabet. John is busy doing some math, and I am writing the "family diary." The snow line is down to the northern limits of the city. It is beautiful. Everything looks so calm. It won't be long, assuming status quo, before we will be skiing. I am currently reading an excellent book: *Nightrunners of Bengal* by John Masters. It concerns the Indian Mutiny in 1857.

12:25 p.m.

Well, so much for tennis; it is still raining. Gordon Griffes came over, so the three of us went for a walk in the rain. We went by the new market, and it was stocked up to the ceiling with food, an encouraging sign. The traffic and people on Saltanatabad, a main street, were "as usual." Saw some Americans on the street, so we stopped and swapped rumors. Nothing new. The Shah is having a big ceremony up at the palace for any who want to wish him well. Probably not much of a crowd. We and the Craigs, our intended tennis opponents, are going over to the Griffeses this afternoon for tacos. Anything to relieve the boredom. John, Tori, and Lynn Griffes are now playing and arguing over a game of Risk.

Dear Mom and Dad,

Well, John and Peggy called last night, and things don't sound too good from their perspective. John and I discussed me taking the kids to England, but it rained last night, and we woke up to snow in the mountains, so maybe I can take the kids skiing until the eighteenth. In any case, I think we will wait it out. Today, we canceled our tennis with the Craigs and the Griffeses, and we are having tacos tonight at the Griffeses. I will get the traveler's checks tomorrow (five hundred dollars) and two hundred dollars more in rials. I worked with the kids on schoolwork this morning. I worry about Tori. She can pick out the letters and spell words for me by looking at the letters. We need to work on letter sounds. Lynn is over playing, and Gordon, John, and little John walked to Super Parmis.

***

Sunday, November 12, 1978

Returned to work. School is still closed until November 18.

Dear Mom and Dad,

Well, I went to Shah Abbas this morning and waited in line for more rials and to buy more film. They were out of traveler's checks again. The lines weren't as bad as last Wednesday. My new maid came today. Her name is Nargas. She seems very good. She moves things when she cleans and really cleans up. She will stay, like "downstairs" Zahari does, until two thirty and will fix lunch. I love the lunches Zahari fixes: hamburger, which smells really good. Our electricity is out, and it has been out for three and a half hours. Rumor has it, the electric workers are on strike, but the Shah Abbas building did have electricity. The phone has been out for twenty minutes. It is still raining, and John and Tori are fighting. Renee has the girls, and Claire and I are splitting forces on the boys. It is all very trying. Claire and I painted in the afternoon, and that helped. John's parents called at seven o'clock. The news coverage in the U.S. on Iran shows more terror and damage than there is. There are times when freedom of the press gets carried away on selling a good story. The poor Shah. He truly is the Greek tragedy. Khomeini has such hatred for him; he doesn't care what damage his followers do to Iran. The Shah's father killed Khomeini's father, and the Shah's army killed his son, so Khomeini is very bitter and vengeful. It doesn't seem to help to talk to our parents. It only makes John and I squabble, so I wash my hair and then feel better.

"A tense calm prevailed Sunday in Tehran where a week ago rampant rioting was touched off by military gunfire that killed as many as 65 students attempting to topple a statue of the Shah.

The anti-Shah National Front, whose leader was jailed Saturday night, claimed its strike against the government was still effective. …

The bazaar in the heart of the city was virtually deserted."[68]

***

Monday, November 13, 1978

Nora's parents called late last night. News headlines say Americans are evacuating Iran, and some cities are on fire. Today, the kids were home again; however, I went to work around eleven this morning. About seventy TCI employees went from floor to floor in our building, demanding the Americans get out and chanting, "We will see you never!" Although there was no physical violence, words were spoken. TCI officials advised us to leave and return when things quieted down. That will probably be tomorrow. As we pulled away from the building, we heard catcalls and clapping. Some Iranians who worked with us were in the crowd and appeared a little embarrassed about the whole incident. By twelve fifteen, I was home.

Mohamodi, one of our taxi drivers, took cooking gas canisters from the Parkers, Corricellos, and us to get them filled. That was yesterday. Today, he returned. There's no cooking gas in all of Tehran, so he had to drive to Karaj twice, which is about sixty miles to the west, to get what we needed. The shortage is due to the problems in the Abadan oil fields.

Last Wednesday, an ABII employee was in a gas line to fill up his Blazer. A few cars started crowding in front of him. Drivers got out of their cars and started arguing while the American just stayed and watched. A policeman arrived with a bullhorn and told the people to disperse, but they continued to argue. The policeman motioned for a soldier to approach. The soldier leveled his rifle and shot three of the Iranians. We don't know how serious they were hurt, but it shows the army means business. More troops arrived shortly, so after waiting in line for two hours, the ABII employee (who stayed in line) filled up the Blazer and went back to work.

Two Bell Helicopter employees were in a cab last week taking pictures of the ravaged areas in Tehran. A soldier told the driver to stop since picture taking was forbidden in the riot areas of the city. The driver apparently did not hear the soldier and continued on; the soldier then shot and killed the driver. The two Bell employees were cut by flying glass but not injured seriously. Just a case of people doing the wrong thing, in the wrong place, at the wrong time. Malek-Abhari, President of TCI, is deliberating whether to request troops to protect the Sepah Square Building. It's the main network center for international calls in and out of Tehran. There have been numerous demonstrations at the building, and some equipment has already been destroyed. At ten o'clock tonight, I found out from my boss, Gordon Griffes, that we will not go to work tomorrow. Since TCI does not know why their employees wanted us out of the building, the company wants us out again tomorrow.

Dear Mom and Dad,

I got a cab early and went to Shah Abbas to get traveler's checks; they were out (surprise, surprise). Then we went down to the commissary by all the burned-out banks. I must say, the demonstrators were very selective in their targets. On Iranshahr Boulevard, only banks were hit. My travel agent and the small stores were untouched. There was a line out in front of the American Consulate, but I was able to bypass the line to go to the commissary. I cashed a check with an ID and purchased seventy-four dollars' worth of canned goods. There is no more liquor. I kept thinking when the electricity is out, if the refrigerator goes, we wouldn't have anything to eat.

When I got home, John walked in. TCI had asked everyone to leave his building; seventy demonstrators had emptied the building! So Steve, Claire, Kathy, John, and I had a beer while the five boys played war and the girls did something else. John made tortilla shells tonight, and we had refried beans, jalapeños, sour cream, and lettuce in burritos. I looked everywhere for a sitter for tomorrow, but TAS is back in session, and I had no luck. Then Gordon called and said John wasn't going to work tomorrow, so he stays home with the kids while I go to work. That is a switch in our house.

***

Tuesday, November 14, 1978

Nora worked today, teaching English to the Iranian Army officers at the Iranian Army Staff College, and I babysat—a switch. Visited the Griffeses today; no work again tomorrow. TCI officials told us to leave the TCI building for good, so we are moving our offices this weekend to the Kakh Street building, the one that burned last week. This probably spells the end of the Status Room and inevitably means new job assignments. There is a rumor that ABII will be cutting its forces back as much as 80 percent, meaning many will have to go home early. It is literally the twilight time for ABII. I heard today several close working peers were going home. So much has happened so quickly. Tonight, we had no electricity for about an hour. From the roof, it appeared the whole northeast side of the city had no power. This has happened before when demonstrators damaged electrical equipment, and it was probably the same thing tonight. I found out tonight that shortly after leaving work yesterday—or rather being forced out—troops arrived at our building. They did a floor-by-floor search and forced all demonstrators out of the building. It's unfortunate we gave in and left so early because it only encourages further demonstrations.

ABII has formed an "Emergency Communication Network" that will be used to pass along information and directions in the event of an emergency. Employees are being asked to notify their supervisor when they will be absent from their place of residence for more than one day. Supervisors are personally responsible for verifying and recording the exact place of residence of their employees.

Dear Mom and Dad,

Well, a typical Iranian morning. I got up and was ready at eight to be picked up to go to work. At 9:15, the first girl they pick up called, and they hadn't come yet. Cute. Yesterday, I spent two hours on the phone trying to find someone who knew someone who could 'sit today. I'm glad I'm not paying a sitter (John is the sitter since he is not at work)! Then I went out to wait, and a car hit the lamp post on the corner. A bus, two cars, and a truck got stuck in the jube ditch trying to pass him. It was an amazing way to spend the forty-five minutes waiting. What they chanted at John yesterday was "We will see you never!" So here we all sit! At ten thirty, the phone rang, and the car is on its way. We got to the college in time for the second class at eleven thirty. I really enjoy going. They are such nice men and really interested in learning English. Today, we discussed helicopters, and I learned a lot. We discussed them for forty-five minutes in English and about ten out of sixteen participated in the discussion, which I guess is good. John isn't going to work tomorrow, so I have a babysitter again. They wondered what happened to me this morning and last week when I didn't teach, but we didn't discuss it much. I just said the embassy advised us to stay home, so we did. No news or papers again today. All Americans now know about ABII not working, so more rumors in the making.

ABII Security

"During the past week, security bulletins were replaced by organizational chain calling due to unscheduled days off and lack of gasoline to make distribution to all buildings.

Activities Last Week:

Last week, employees were given two days off work because of demonstrations.

In Tehran, three apartment buildings occupied by Americans that work for Boeing, Mobile Oil, and the U.S. Government were firebombed. All damage was minor, and no injuries were reported.

In Isfahan, two unoccupied vehicles belonging to Bell Helicopter were burned.

Other News:

National Front Leader Sanjabi, who called a national strike a few weeks ago, was arrested just prior to addressing foreign correspondents. He was accused with conducting anti-state activities. What effect his arrest will have on the situation here in Iran is not known. Sanjabi had been in Paris the past few weeks, conferring with Emam Khomeini.

Yesterday, approximately 40 employees went through TCI Microwave, TCI Stores, TCI Main, and TCI No. 2 buildings asking ABII employees to leave the buildings, which they did in order to avoid a confrontation. ABII employees will not return to these buildings until a solution is worked out between Messrs. Kertz, Bartlett, and Malek-Abhari. There was no physical violence used or threatened yesterday.

As of this date, only 30 ABII dependents and two employees have left Iran because of the political unrest.

Security Briefings:

In order to keep upper management advised of the day-to-day situation, I give a daily briefing to Messrs. Kertz and Bartlett. I am also in daily contact with the U.S. Embassy, U.S. Air Force investigators, other businesses, and the local police. Based on the information received, measures have been taken to ensure the safety of our employees and their dependents—such as moving employees in the provinces from an impending disturbance, alerting employees of potential problem areas, and reinforcing security at office buildings.

A Look Ahead:

After the recent martial law crackdown, life in Tehran appears to be getting back to normal. In the meantime, Messrs. Kertz and Bartlett as well as the ABII Security personnel will make every effort to keep employees informed by issuing security bulletins, chain calling, or any other appropriate means."[69]

***

Wednesday, November 15, 1978

No work again today. At one thirty, Griffes's whole group met at the 21 Complex for a meeting. We discussed the moving plan from the TCI building to the Kakh Street building. All moving will have to be done over the weekend. When I got home, I took the skis out and adjusted the bindings. The snow level is very low, and the mountains are beckoning us.

This was left on my desk today (original spelling and grammar preserved):

"Don't Come, Yankee go home.
Gentleman:
We, the staff of Directorate General of Telecommunications, request you not to show up in this Directorate office from Saturday morning 18 November1978.We desire you a very happy life in your own country the U.S.A."

Dear Mom and Dad,
Today I went to work at eight, and John was home with the kids and the maid. I loved leaving him with the maid, a Farsi translation book, a hungry Tori, and a mad John. School seemed very long. I had a sore throat when I started and felt sick by the time I got home. I enjoy the class because they all have a sense of humor. Our talk today was on Chinook helicopters. I am learning so much about helicopters, 210 Chinook, Huey, etc. My other class follows the book pretty much. I told them about the Planning Commission in Pleasant Hill, and they thought it sounded too bureaucratic. I came home and went to bed.

John says he is staying at TCI-2, but all the other ABII units will go to Kakh Street. That is the building that was attacked and burned. So John and seven others are the only Americans left in the eleven-story TCI-2 building. I wonder how long they will let them stay. The news says the oil strike is over, but there are no papers and no American Women's Club handbooks. I think the mail is working again.

Things have been exciting around here as I am sure you have heard. However, the American press gets an A+ in sensationalism on this one. One article said, "The tanks surrounded the desolate streets of Tehran as the whole city was a smoldering heap" [source is no longer available]. Tehran is as large as Los Angeles, and that is a lot of tanks! Actually, it was just the downtown business section that was hit Sunday. They were amazingly selective; liquor stores, banks, and foreign businesses got it. ABII's Kakh Street building was evacuated and burned. Buses and cars were burned. School was canceled for two weeks. We have no newspapers, as the press was destroyed by either the new military government or the rioters. There has been no local news until today on TV. Stores were out of food and candles for a few days. John has been home four days because of problems. School kept kids overnight because the buses couldn't get through the rioters, and many people are leaving the city. However, my life really seems quite normal. Other than the fact we have to be home at nine o'clock for curfew and everything is canceled including Catholic Church religion class, nothing seems unusual. Iranians are all very friendly to me. During the food scare, I had a koochek (small) store hide eggs for me. I think I paid two dollars for a dozen. A cab driver drove to Karaj for cooking gas for me, and my officers at school were very glad to see me come back.

I am teaching English at the Army Staff Command College. I really love it. If all goes right, a car picks me up at 8:15 a.m., I teach for four hours, and I'm home by two. The kids get home at three when they are in school (which is iffy nowadays). I earn about twenty-eight dollars a day, and I work two days a week. The students are majors and colonels in the army. Most of them have been to the States, but they ask the weirdest questions. "What is a lap?" "What is static and fluctuation on a radio?" "What is the difference between in time and on time?" We have a speech each day from one officer, so I am learning a lot about helicopters, as some are pilots. The only problem is the school is located about one mile from Tehran University, where much of the action takes place. Thank goodness we have a plainclothes driver, and he drives a station wagon, or I think we would be nervous. Some of my friends think I am crazy, but I still say Iranians like "blondes."

John has been home to babysit, so the Iranians kicked ABII out of his building. They are moving all ABII employees down to Kakh Street (the building that was burned earlier), but John and seven others are to stay behind. I wonder if they will let him stay there. We will see Saturday. The night after the big riot, after curfew when the embassy told us to stay indoors the next day, little John got an ear infection. Thank God I had some penicillin on hand. The school for the kids, Piruzi, is great when it is open. John is learning French and Tori is learning some other language. The school had a celebration day where each class did a skit representing different countries, mothers made cookies from all over the world, and they flew flags from every nation.

They also sang the Iranian national anthem and "Happy Birthday" to the Shah. Obviously, this was a few weeks ago. Now, I have heard they don't fly the flag or sing the anthem. They canceled sports and have tanks and guards on every street. But the kids don't ask questions or know what is happening. They do practice drills where they drop to the floors in case of rioters. Piruzi hasn't had any trouble, but schools in the south part of the city have. I am taking a ballet class still.

My photography class was canceled until January. Our trip to Greece was great, and I am glad we went. I am painting but not nudes, as there are no models here. It is hard to get a model without a chador. Thanks for thinking of us with packages, but the mail is so screwed up it really isn't worth the effort. Thanks again for writing.

Daughter Tori's letter to her friend Kristin (Tori was five).

Dear Kristin,

How are you doing? I won't wear dresses. I wear John's jeans. I am listening to Alice in Wonderland. We don't get TV until 7:00 p.m. Dad is fixing my skis. We will ski soon. I haven't lost any teeth yet. We are having fun. Ask Toddy's mother to come to Tehran with Todd and Scott. I let Mom brush my hair. Mom bought me a camel necklace. I really like it. I have lots of friends: Amy, Frank, Leslie, Katherine, Jonathan, Dante, Lisa, Robin, Bret, and Clark, but I miss you. What are you learning at school? I make pumpkins and witches and know the alphabet. I won't let Mom comb my hair again for one day.

Love, Tori

***

Thursday, November 16, 1978

We went to the Corricellos for a very nice dinner with the Parkers. We were home by nine. Nora had a cold all day.

***

Friday, November 17, 1978

We had lunch with the Dyers at the Pars Club followed by window shopping. Tried to call my parents, but the satellite lines were down.

Dear Mom and Dad,

Today we went to ten thirty Catholic Mass. Father Williams, the eighty-year-old priest, said he went to an embassy meeting yesterday, and they don't know what is going on either. But damn it, the dumb Boy Scouts are meeting Monday, and Kathy is dropping out, so I'm the new den leader—darn. Civil war breaks out, and I worry about milk cartons to make bird feeders and how to conjugate the verb "to be." Kathy took the kids to an ABII-Bell Helicopter football game, so John and I had a nice walk. Gordon called, and everything is so screwed up, John doesn't have to go to work tomorrow. ABII moved out of TCI-2 (except John's group) to the Kakh Street building, but the existing tenants didn't move out of Kakh Street, so no one has an office. We may go to the bazaar. The kids will be in school for one day, then a holiday, followed by two days in school, then another holiday—what a joke. Then Ashura holy period hits the first week of December, so they will probably be home again. I feel like one needs the patience of Job to cope over here these days. My John has been home six days out of the last ten just because everything is so screwed up.

***

Saturday, November 18, 1978

It was my first day of work since November 13. Everything appeared normal; although, the Kakh building move was a mess with all the extra people milling around. The Iranians who worked with us seemed to harbor no resentment toward us. Most of ABII has moved from the TCI building. Our small group is staying with a few others; out of an original group of around two hundred employees, about twenty-five are left. If an employee feels their life is in danger, he or she will be reassigned to a new job at the Kakh building. Only one woman felt that way, so she had been reassigned. The army had moved in and stationed troops outside the building, all carrying rifles with bayonets. They also had two .50 caliber machine guns mounted on the back of two trucks facing the street.

Today, Webster, the staff supervisor of the Status Room, submitted a list of employees for our group. ABII employees in TCI-2 room 717 were W.J. Van De Mark, A.G. Hedrick, N.D. Siganporia, and L.J. Cox. The employees in room 718 were G.R. Tears, J.B. Doolittle, R.D. Barth, and M.L. Leach.

Dear Mom and Dad,

Hi. We got your letter of October 31 today, November 18, so the mail is getting better. School started again today after a two-week recess. While John was home a lot during the past two weeks, we are all still here together and happy.

I am still teaching at the Army Staff College, and I really enjoy it. We don't discuss women's rights, religion, or politics, but everything else is fair game. Yes, John's Star Wars figures arrived. I'm sorry I didn't send you a thank you note. Don't use the APO number. We haven't received anything using that address. Remember, don't send any packages through the regular mail. We will miss seeing you on Thanksgiving. We are having the Griffeses and Mike Terry over. Send us your newspaper clippings on Iran. We love reading about us, as we have no newspapers now. We are hoping to go to Amsterdam March 15–April 6. We have a car and hotel accommodations. We will spend most of our time in Switzerland, Germany, and France. John and Tori will be with us the whole three weeks. The best news about all our problems is the Cub Scouts are canceled until January, so I won't have to be den leader. My art show is canceled for December. Our ballet classes might fold. Camera class is canceled. Thank goodness for my teaching job and the snow in the mountains. We should start skiing next month. John wants to go see a Walt Disney movie at the Tehran American Society on the thirtieth, which is when we are celebrating his birthday. I hope it works out. They don't have the films yet. They are hung up in customs. Inshallah or "Allah Willing" is the way this place functions these days. Claire and I looked for a week for our Thanksgiving turkeys; we are having cranberry salad, cranberry sauce, stuffing, turkey, and pumpkin pie. How about that? We will miss seeing you on the holidays. Tori's card is supposed to say, "Thank you for my birthday money. I bought a bicycle from Brent Dwyer with it." In closing, this letter took so long to write, as I never could get stamps.

ABII Notice

"There is little doubt that these past few weeks have been trying ones. Much of the current 'Iran Experience' is probably different than what you expected when you decided to accept the intrigues and challenges of living in a foreign country.

Recently, some dependents and employees have opted to return to their former homes and companies. Each family faces challenges in its own unique way, for its own personal reasons. How one family reacts to a given situation by no means sets a standard for another family to follow. This is a fact that I appreciate and respect.

I do want to assure each of you that your company is vitally concerned about your welfare. We are in constant communication with the U.S. Embassy, other foreign businesses, and local social leaders to continually assess the current unrest. We are constantly creating and revising contingency plans for every conceivable situation that may develop. In every case, our employees and families are top priority.

Hopefully, the unrest will soon quiet down, and we will have weathered the storm. But in the meantime, I ask for your support. Keep cool, and don't be influenced or unduly concerned by false rumors that spread like brush fires in these kinds of situations.

In turn, we will do our best to keep you up to date on what is happening. We will continue to issue bulletins at work, use the telephone, and any other means of communication that best fits the situation. I remind you that our Security Organization is the best source for getting facts and checking out rumors. We also have an Information Line during business hours at Shah Abbas, Ext. 2207.

If you have questions requiring individual attention, please have the employee-spouse contact his or her supervisor who can either help or provide direction to those who can.

Thank you,
W.E. Bartlett
Executive Vice President—Iran"[70]

***

Sunday, November 19, 1978

This is a holiday. I played tennis with Gordon Griffes.

"The Iranian government released 210 political prisoners and Shah Mohammad Reza Pahlavi renewed his pledge of two weeks ago to hold free elections next June and bring an end to the military rule he imposed on the country."[71]

***

Tuesday, November 21, 1978

Today, I requested a minibus each Thursday for transportation to ski areas (Shemshak or Dizin) for John, Nora, John, and Tori Doolittle and Steve, Claire, Frank, Amy, and Leslie Parker, all residing at Koocheh Mariam Number Six. I also asked the same for Ken, Rene, Lisa, and Dante Corricello at 18 Naz (Hatef Esphani). In the request, I stated our work group had not moved, so I planned to be here indefinitely. A map to both locations was forwarded. Played tennis with Nora in the evening.

ABII Security

"Arrangements have been made with the American Consulate for ABII employees to send and receive emergency telegrams to and from the United States. In order to take advantage of this opportunity, the employee or dependent should go to the American Consulate to see Mr. Sorenson, who is responsible for the American Services Section.

Mr. Sorenson will arrange to have the telegram sent and also receive a reply from the U.S. The cost of this service is $15 for a one-way telegram or $30 for a telegram to and from the U.S. The hours of operation are from 8:00 a.m. to 12:00 noon and from 2:00 to 4:00 p.m.

The AT&T switchboard operators in New York have been advised to refer emergency calls and information calls from families in the U.S. to Hadley Road. Urgent information will be relayed to Iran by radio circuits."[72]

ABII Notice

"Due to the current situation in Iran, limiting the shipment of personal effects to the CONUS [Continental United States] to one will be temporarily waived. One partial shipment of personal effects is authorized to the area of your past Bell System assignment."[73]

"Wildcat strikes by power workers…cut electricity in several sections of the capital and created panic among residents who feared the shutdown would cause a water shortage.

The strike shut down businesses and caused panicky Tehran residents to fill every available container with water in the event electricity was cut to central pumping stations.

The shutdowns followed threats by the electricity workers earlier in the week they would throw the switches as a protest against censorship of television and radio shows—the only source of information still functioning since newspaper employees walked off the job two weeks ago over the same issue."[74]

***

Wednesday, November 22, 1978

My parents called, concerned.

ABII Notice

"ABII currently has a limited supply of cooking gas.

Requests to have one tank delivered to your apartment may be placed as follows: [detail provided]. There must be someone at the apartment to accept delivery. Tanks will not be left in hallways, etc.

This is a temporary procedure and will be discontinued when normal deliveries start."[75]

"Troops opened fire on anti-shah demonstrators in Tehran's bazaar…and heavy tanks rolled into the capital for the first time in 11 days in a swift crackdown to head off further outbursts. …

Witnesses said 200 demonstrators paraded through the bazaar's narrow, twisting streets shouting slogans against the shah and Azhari[the Military Premier General] and praising Ayatollah Khomeini, the exiled Iranian religious leader who has demanded the shah's abdication. ...

At least nine British-made heavy Chieftain tanks, brought to Tehran after rioting November 5 laid waste to vast areas of the capital, took up positions along the bazaar's perimeter road, and troops set up machine gun posts.

The tanks' 155-mm gun barrels pointed at the bazaar's tiny shops, where witnesses said storefronts displayed pictures of Khomeini, but none of the shah."[76]

***

Thursday, November 23, 1978

Nora's parents called, concerned about what's happening politically. The Griffeses and Mike Terry came over. Played some tennis with Gordon later in the day.

Dear Mom and Dad,

Thank you for the phone call. I am sorry we haven't been able to get through for awhile. I also ran out of stamps and couldn't find time to get more while teaching. I love my job; thank goodness I have it. It keeps me busy, and all the men are so nice. We discussed Vietnam and American geography today for our "speeches" and the difference between six and sex. They always try to throw me with shockers, but their shockers are so mild. Our Thanksgiving table seated eleven. It was Joan's little blue-and-white Isfahan tablecloth over Tori's blue sheets, including the fitted sheet. We had the Griffeses, Mike Terry, Terry Scott, and a few others over.

***

Friday, November 24, 1978

Attended the TAS football game. It is John's ninth birthday! We plan to celebrate it November 30.

Dear Mom and Dad,

John is melting wax from one candle into another to save the wax. We are running low, as that is our only source of light and heat for four hours a night. This is all so unreal, but we have good friends and are all in the same boat, so we can manage. We had a nice Thanksgiving. We got a thirty-three-dollar, fourteen-pound turkey the day before and felt thankful to get a turkey at all. Everyone was excited about one can of cranberry sauce for ten people and a salad with crushed pineapple and cranberries. The kids are adjusting quite well. They play games, do homework, read, and chase back and forth among four apartments, so we muddle along. They all know the chant of the protesters and guess when the electricity will go off. We saw a Jeep with soldiers and a machine gun on the way home from church, and little John said, "Well, Mom, they just want to make sure they [the demonstrators] don't overturn cars." The things we accept as commonplace now would be considered unreal at home.

***

Saturday, November 25, 1978

Demonstrations downtown today. Some Iranians were killed by army troops.

***

Sunday, November 26, 1978

10:00 a.m.

Troops have been in front of our building for the last two weeks. Today, TCI security came into the building and arrested some more individuals for their part in the force-out last week. The remaining TCI employees left their jobs and walked down to the lobbies of both TCI buildings in protest. People started catcalling and clapping at the troops; paper was thrown out the windows. More troops arrived along with the riot police. Employees in the mall between the two buildings formed into masses, shouting and waving up to the others in the TCI buildings

117

for them to join the strike with those outside. However, soldiers forced the crowd to disperse.

One person was reluctant and started running between the buildings. Two soldiers started chasing him. One leveled his rifle and told the employee to stop. Another soldier blocked his way, stopped him, and started kicking him and beating him around the head. The employee threw his hands up in submission. The soldiers continued to kick him, and one butt-stroked him in the head. After some questioning by an army officer, the employee walked away with a bandage on the back of his head. More soldiers showed up, and the TCI employees finally dispersed, walked out of the area and away from their jobs. Including today, thirty-eight TCI employees have been arrested by the police and TCI security forces for the force-out of ABII a week ago. Some have been arrested for anti-Shah activities.

12:00 p.m.

Things have quieted down. The employees have either gone home or returned to their job locations. Those who returned to their jobs are still not working in protest to today's action and a previously declared strike. It is apparent many man-hours have been lost during the past few weeks. The employees, even when on strike, still get paid. Because of this, there is little incentive to settle and return to work. An Iranian coworker brought his entire family to work, spread out a blanket, and read, played games, and drank tea. There is no apparent anti-Americanism. Most of the complaints of the TCI employees center on TCI management and the Shah. One cannot help but wonder when things are going to return to normal. There is a rumor that the Kakh Street building group is going to be disbanded. We all wonder what this means.

There is no mail today because the Shah Abbas mail employees forgot we are still working in our old building. We found out today the United States Commissary is no longer going to be open. The commissary was a big plus for us. Because I was still in the Air Force Reserves (taking correspondence courses), we could get food and liquor there. Alas, no more.

***

Monday, November 27, 1978

A quiet day at work. I came home to find John had tried to use my reel-to-reel tape deck to play some music, and there was tape all over the floor. I was upset, but then I decided to teach him how to use it properly. He enjoyed listening to Led Zeppelin!

***

Tuesday, November 28, 1978

Work as usual today. Went to the Kakh Street building to work on a Statement of Work project for Gordon. That was the first time in several weeks I have really "worked." We are busy trying to justify to the Iranians all the tasks ABII should have "allocated man-hours" for. The more tasks they cut, the fewer ABII employees will be needed. Today, I also filled out my Semi-Monthly Iran Personal Safety and Security Update.

I found out today the mayor of San Francisco, George Moscone, had been killed. What a shock: not only violence in Iran, but even at home! We ate dinner by candlelight.

The flyer below was left on my desk at work. I have no idea who the writer is or who the intended audience is. I included this because it seemed to fit with all I had heard at this time.

"The U.S. Embassy held a routine briefing…and updated us on the present situation.

I. The situation in Tehran remains relatively stable, despite intermittent demonstrations and strikes, while in the provinces, things are more volatile, especially in those areas where there is no martial law and limited military support available.

A. There were two demonstrations in the city during the morning, one at Shah Reza and Ferdowsi, and one on Saltanatabad. No injuries were reported.

B. There was a gathering on Fakhrabad involving approximately 40 people yesterday afternoon.

119

C. In Isfahan in the past few days, there have been several incidents of fires and car burnings, and curfew has been moved to 2000 [8:00 p.m.].

D. Demonstrations and incidents of violence have been reported in G'rgan, Sari Kermanshah, and Rasht. Numerous large demonstrations have been occurring in Mashhad, but no violence has been reported.

II. Muharram is expected to be a period of increased activity; although, the embassy cannot foresee the extent of the 'shelough.'

A. More assemblies and strikes are likely, and a possible general strike is predicted.

B. You should maintain a low profile, especially on December 10 and 11, the most solemn of the Moslem holidays.

1. Do NOT take photographs of the processions if they occur.

2. Do NOT have parties, but if you MUST, don't party in groups of more than 10.

3. Keep all music low.

III. Strikes continue in some sectors.

A. There is continued trouble at NIOC (National Iranian Oil Company), with occasional demonstrations and sit-ins.

B. The Ministry of Finance is still on strike.

C. The customs is still out.

D. High schools and universities are not expected to resume classes until 1979.

E. There is no end in sight to the newspaper strike.

IV. Continued shortages may occur.

A. It is possible that during Muharram, a general strike may be called to last several days.

B. It would be wise to stock up on essentials since shops may be closed for an extended period.

C. Bottled gas production should be back at its former level within three days or so, but because of a pipeline problem, it may be a couple of weeks before the capsule supply is back to normal.

D. Petrol is back at almost 100% production, but there are still distribution problems. Tehran is experiencing a run on gasoline because of a combination of a variety of factors.
   1. There is a shortage of stock in Tehran district.
   2. People fear further power outages will interfere with pumping activity.
   3. People fear national strike.
   4. There is a refinery strike of small proportions in Rey.
   5. NIOC is undergoing difficulties.

V. Harassment of foreigners has not abated, but not increased.
   A. Telephone calls, painted slogans, letters, and leaflets are still being received by members of the foreign community.
   B. Some people have had their car tires slashed.
   C. Those who have had their cars burned in Isfahan have not been recipients of threatening notes.

VI. Travel and currency exchange are restricted.
   A. Casual travel in the provinces is discouraged.
   B. Travelers may exchange up to 200,000 rials per passport per trip.
      1. You must show your passport and all your travel documents when making the exchange.
      2. The information will be entered in your passport, and it is expected that bank officials will check your passport for exit and entry stamps before making an additional exchange.
   C. The exchange dealers are doing a booming business, and you may change money with them.
      1. Their exchange is 76 rials per $1.00 selling dollars.
      2. Their exchange is 78–79 rials per $1.00 buying dollars.
      3. Bank Melli's official rate is 71 and 72.5.
   D. There are no searches for money at the airport and no actual limit to the amount you may leave the country with.
   E. There is a rial cash shortage because there has been a recent run on the banks, and they are now rationing their supply of rials.

VII. Other rumors await verification.
   A. Iran Air is said to be going on strike for 20 days starting today, but there is no confirmation of this.

121

B. No information is forthcoming regarding any change in curfew hours.

C. Lockheed has NOT issued a Code +/- 1[an evacuation status] and knows less than we do, according to a wife of one of their employees."[77]

ABII Security

"During the past week, there have been civil disorders both in Tehran and in the provinces. In Tehran last weekend, two United States Government employees' cars were burned just off Saltanatabad. On Sunday November 26, there were five demonstrations in different sections of the city and a strike which resulted in the shutdown of 70% of the businesses, including gas stations. Demonstrators numbered 50 to 300. There were no reported casualties or injuries.

In Isfahan, demonstrations during the past week have resulted in both injuries and casualties—none to Americans. On Sunday, November 26, a large group of demonstrators burned three banks and several buildings. As a result of these demonstrations, the curfew was changed to 8:00 p.m. to 6:00 a.m. At approximately 8:15p.m., the first night under the new curfew, a U.S. military officer's house was firebombed. The damage was severe; however, no personal injuries were sustained.

It is possible that the oil refineries may shut down beginning December 2 through December 10. It is felt that during this time period, we will experience several strikes beginning December 2, which could possibly curtail services including gasoline deliveries to service stations. It is recommended that each employee assigned a company vehicle keep the gas tank full and only use the vehicle for official business during the next ten-day period. Should an emergency exist, these vehicles will be the only source of transportation available for ABII employees and dependents. Employees should also make sure that they have their heating oil at a level that will carry them through the next two weeks. If the strike in the oil field materializes, it is expected that the heating oil supply will be limited. Employees should take necessary precautions to ensure that they have an adequate food supply that would last for at least one week should these strikes close down the normal supply of commodities.

It is recommended that all employees and dependents continue to maintain a low profile through the upcoming religious period from December 2 through December 11. This will include elimination of any personal travel in Iran for this time period. All business travel out of Tehran has been cancelled for the next two weeks. Should any additional information concerning the above become available during the next few days, it will be relayed to our employees immediately."[78]

***

Wednesday, November 29, 1978

No electricity last night, so we ate dinner by candlelight. Tonight, the Parkers had about forty people over for Christmas carols, hot wine, and finger food. A diversion! I requested some information in case I want to send Nora, John, and Tori home until the present situation improves.

***

Thursday, November 30, 1978

John's birthday celebration was today. We were supposed to take ten kids to the Tehran American Society to see a movie called *The Computer Wore Tennis Shoes*, but upon checking, we found out the movie was still in customs due to a customs strike. So instead, we entertained with games, cake, and comic books. All had a good time.

The Parkers and Nora and I had the Dryers for dinner. Kathy is leaving for good on December 1, and Ken is following three weeks later. Nora will really miss Kathy. She has been a very close friend and confidant. Electricity went out again tonight. The demonstrators boast about having the power to turn the electricity off and on at their whim. And they do.

***

Friday, December 1, 1978

Played tennis with John Noske today; I beat him 6–3, 7–5. He was the one who beat Gordon and me over the summer, playing with his son. Tonight, we went to a going away party for Dave Bender from ABII, who's going home. Dave lived with Terry Scott and Mike Terry. We enjoyed the diversion from the normal "low profile" action. Kathy Dyer left today, and Nora was upset. I don't blame her. There was much gunfire in the city tonight. For the next eleven days, the Iranians observe a very sad holy period. They go about beating themselves with chains and chanting. Television has gone off the air for fifteen days, and the radio is playing only classical music. There is no paper, no news, no nothing. All we have is the "rumor mill."

It rained early this morning, and now there's snow in the mountains, so skiing may be in the future. We still don't know what is happening with ABII. Perhaps we will have to go home, perhaps not. As long as the kids are in school, Nora is able to work, and we are safe, we will stay.

ABII Notice

"Demonstrations after curfew in southeast Tehran resulted in military and police activity. Gunfire was heard for approximately two hours. Embassy reports 30 people injured and eight dead. No Americans were involved."[79]

"Government troops fired machine guns for more than three hours…killing at least seven persons and crushing a demonstration by thousands of Moslem mourners, many of them wrapped in white shrouds, who poured into the streets in suicidal defiance of the military curfew gripping Iran. …

The Moslems streamed into the streets shouting, 'Death of the shah!' and 'Allah Akbar!' (God is great) only hours after Ayatollah Ruhollah Khomeini, the shah's archenemy, called on his Moslem followers to 'sacrifice your blood to overthrow the tyrant.'…

Ambulance sirens wailed after intermittent bursts of machine-gun and automatic rifle fire were heard in a widespread downtown district from the Grand Bazaar to the Zaleh square in east Tehran, scene of the 'Black Friday' army shooting on September 8 that killed at least 250 people."[80]

***

Saturday, December 2, 1978

The following was left on my desk. It was in both English and Farsi (the original spelling and punctuation has been maintained).

"To the foreigners, whose government supports, somehow or another the government of shah. No doubt you are aware of the present liberating movement of Iranian nation. Our goal, in general, is to get rid of the internal autocratic monarchy and external exploitation. We want to build an Islamic Republic in Iran, so as to be able to think freely and gain freedom and independence the basis of justice and then base our relations with other nation's _ding to mutual respect and fairness. Knowingly or unknowingly you are working for the benefits of our nation's enemy, some how or another; so your presence in Iran is considered as an obstacle for our Revolution. So you and your family one month period to leave this country. Then action to take all the remaining foreigners as our enemies and fight them off categorically. Due to the understanding manner of french people and goodness towards our High Religious figure, Emam KHOMAINY the french will be safe for the time being and also all foreign journalists will be excepted. We have asked all our people to prepare, according to their possib_ a list of addresses of foreigners, foreign Firms and Companies of this district and working place prepare themselves for struggle.(signed) University Pand for Islamic Republic in Iran"

10:00 a.m.

We just heard the Tehran American School and Community School have closed for the day due to the trouble last night and the continuing trouble downtown. If Piruzi School closes, I am sure Nora will want to go home. Mr. Bartlett, ABII's vice president, is holding a special meeting tomorrow for all nonworking wives—probably going to try and stem the tide of departing spouses and do a little morale boosting. I heard from Mr. Afkari, an Iranian TCI employee, that TCI employees will go on strike today in protest of all the killings last night. The electricity went off from midtown north, which affected us.

10:30 a.m.

TCI employees are walking out at the Kakh and Takhte Tavoos buildings in protest to the killings by the soldiers (rumor estimates the number at fifteen thousand).Troops are in front of our building but are only watching so far. There is a lot of shooting south of Koursh-e-Kabir. I just found out there's no school for TAS again tomorrow, and Mr. Bartlett's meeting for tomorrow has been canceled. Americans are to keep away from public places.

2:30 p.m.

Buses have arrived early in case we have to leave the building in a hurry. The prime minister of Iran is on the Iranian radio station asking everyone to stay inside and obey curfew from nine at night to five in the morning since last night's killings were the result of people marching after the deadline. A few fires have started downtown; I can see the smoke from my window. Many people have been killed today, and the troops had a major confrontation south of Sepah Square. The only utility working well is the telephone company. Without telephones, there would be mass confusion. The electricity just came back on. Looks like tonight may be another violent night.

6:00 p.m.

There's no TV again, and the radio is only in Farsi. At six thirty, the TV came on for fifteen minutes, allowing an Iranian to give an international news summary. He stated there were many killings in the city last night and during the day today.

10:00 p.m.

We heard semiautomatic gunfire and chanting from our home. The shooting seemed fairly close, probably on Dowlat or Koursh-e-Kabir boulevard. All of us went to the roof with the Parkers and their kids. To the north of the city, we could see one fire. The sounds of rifle and machine-gun fire interrupted our thoughts every five or ten minutes. There were many people on the roofs around ours, some chanting or yelling "Allah Akbar!" We could hear tank treads clanking on the street about two blocks away but could see nothing. By eleven, things had quieted down.

ABII Notice

"Small demonstrations occurred in various sections of Tehran. Troops were reported to be firing over the heads of demonstrators to disperse them. As a result of the December 1 event, the U.S. Embassy issued the following alert:

- Exercise extreme caution.
- TAS and Community Schools closed through December 3.
- Dependents should stay home.
- If you have to go out, avoid crowds and stay out of south Tehran.
- Embassy will continue to advise."[81]

"Heavy shooting erupted across Tehran for the second consecutive night Saturday as troops battled thousands of demonstrators who tried to storm the U.S. Embassy and swarmed the streets in defiance of a curfew, chanting the Koran and shouting, 'Down with the shah!'

Sporadic shooting continued until after 2 a.m. Sunday but later the downtown area of the capital appeared calmer.

There was no clear count of casualties at the end of one of the worst days of violence since the campaign to topple the shah began a year ago. Earlier Saturday, official reports said seven people were killed and 35 injured. But the opposition National Front spokesman said there were at least 67 fatalities and demonstrators claimed the toll was much higher.

Angry mobs beat a policeman to death on a Tehran street and troops beat up three reporters—two of them representatives of Newsweek and one a newsman for the London Daily Telegraph—when they left their hotel after curfew to see what was happening in the streets. They were released after a few hours."[82]

***

Sunday, December 3, 1978

I went to work, but the kids stayed home from school. There was no electricity at home or at work, and it was raining hard this morning. On the way, I noticed many black flags hanging at the doors of business establishments. Some said, "They have killed your brother," and others said, "They have killed your sister.""They" meant the army troops. There was little traffic on the way to work. With the rain, the lack of traffic, and the black flags, the feeling was strange. I could hear "Allah Akbar" being yelled from roof to roof as the bus moved along. The people are tired of corruption, imprisonment, and despotism of the Shah. With all the killing, it seems a change in the government must take place, or many more will be killed.

At ten, while the kids were in bed, Nora and I crept up to the roof. Still without electricity, it was dark except for the candles we could see in some of the neighbors' windows. We could hear gunfire and demonstrators chanting. Eventually, it started to rain, but the yells and shooting continued.

ABII Notice

"ABII EMPLOYEES AND FAMILIES,

I regret that the informational meeting scheduled for December 3 for ABII nonworking dependents was postponed. But, as you can appreciate during these times, schedules and plans are subject to change at a moment's notice. So we improvise and try it another way as best we can. Hopefully, until we can reschedule another meeting, this letter may contain information helpful to you and your family.

I have been informed that many of our casual work force expressed concern that they were not included in the scheduled meeting. But, as an important part of the ABII work force, I have felt the normal information flow would have provided them with much of the subject matter of this meeting. I am concerned that all employees receive timely information from their supervisors and will be making a special effort to

128

stress the importance of including our casual employees in the normal information flow to all of our ABII management team.

We're foreigners in a country that is undergoing growing pains. And we're finding out firsthand just how this affects our lives, both on and off the job. Personally, I sum it up with one word: <u>frustration</u>. Frustration for me at work, and frustration for my wife at home. I'm sure it is the same with most of you and your families. There is no getting around the fact that we're faced with trying times, times that will test what we are made of.

ABII is facing a serious challenge that involves us all. Because ABII is nothing more than its employees, it is important now, more than ever before, that these employees get all the support possible, especially from their husbands, wives, and other family members.

I meet often with American Embassy officials. At these meetings, the ambassador shares his security information and opinions. One of the principal points that the ambassador has made is that there are no indications that the situation in Iran is critical enough that American workers here, or their dependents, should be sent home. If a company, or someone personally, elects to take that action, it is a matter of their own choice, not one that is recommended by the embassy. Should a really dire situation develop, the embassy will evacuate all Americans. ABII has a staff of people continually working on procedures to coordinate with the embassy's evacuation plans for evacuation of ABII employees and their families. You are probably aware of this because of the several questionnaires you've received lately, updating our personnel records. An emergency personnel contact plan has been set up by zones so that everyone can be reached, even if telephone lines are disrupted. Ham operators in each zone are also prepared to assist in the plan.

For those who are concerned about their personal property, we've set up a program which permits partial shipment of your household goods back to the States should you decide that would be in your best interest.

As was anticipated, December is going to be a trying month. I would like to cover a few of the precautionary measures suggested by the embassy that we should be taking at the present time:

1. If necessary for women to be outside the apartment, conservative dress is certainly in order.

2. Parties and loud music obviously draw attention at a time when we do not need it.
3. To the extent possible, nonworking dependents should curtail travel about the city as much as possible.
4. During this period, we will be exposed to more and more demonstrations; sounds of gunfire may also become more frequent—when this happens, make sure you remain inside, away from windows, and off of rooftops.
5. Iranians are going through tremendous turmoil in their lives at this time. Even though we are sharing some of this experience with them, I am sure we cannot fully appreciate their situation. We, too, are going through trying times. However, I would encourage you to be mindful that this is when tempers run high, and we will be called on to exhibit more patience in our dealings with the people we encounter.

Really, we are asking you to keep your low profile even lower. In any case, take the recommendations seriously. This doesn't mean stopping all activities. It means avoiding areas where trouble may occur, staying out of the way of disturbances. We'll do our best to keep you informed ahead of time.

Whatever develops this month might well be the last of the serious disruptions. My personal feelings based on the official information I have received are that after December, a return to normalcy can be expected. Meanwhile, if you have concerns or questions regarding our personal safety or welfare, call one of the emergency or information numbers listed each week in *Dear ABII*.

Rumors run rampant during uneasy times. I know. I've been filling buckets with water and emptying them right along with the rest of you. I also share your problem with bottled gas. Hopefully, our new distribution plan for employees has helped.

Besides your personal safety here in Iran, you probably have a real concern for your economic security as well. As you are probably aware, ABII is currently renegotiating its contract with the Imperial Government of Iran. There will undoubtedly be many program curtailments. What they will be and who will be affected isn't known at this time and won't be known until the details are worked out. They may take weeks and perhaps months.

I assure you that when I have this information, I'll share it with you. Until then, let's continue to work together to perform the best job possible under the circumstances.

W.E. Bartlett, Executive Vice President-Iran"[83]

"Imperial troops fired into the air and used tear gas in battles throughout Tehran with thousands of anti-shah demonstrators…

Power went out in many areas of the capital after the shooting started, and the fighting continued in darkness.

There were no immediate reports of casualties. Large groups of demonstrators, many clad in white shrouds that signify their willingness to die, rallied in as many as 25 locations in the capital, officials reported."[84]

***

Monday, December 4, 1978

Electricity continued to be off from noon to four and from ten at night until we went to bed. No school again. We could still hear shooting and chanting throughout the day and night. We listened to the news, as we do every night, on the British Broadcasting Company (BBC) station. It was reported that the Shah was holding many meetings at the palace. Reports also said that a police station in Tehran was attacked by saboteurs using Russian-made machine guns (as evidenced by the shell casings left behind).One policeman was killed.

***

Tuesday, December 5, 1978

For the last two nights, there has been chanting and gunfire. The chanting starts at the mosques and spreads from rooftop to rooftop, telling people to either praise God or take to the streets. All this is done after curfew, so those who go into the streets know they will encounter troops and possible death. Yesterday, a copy of a photograph of a dead Iranian youth was being passed around at work among the Iranians. The picture was being distributed throughout the city to see if anyone could identify him for proper burial. The number of black flags hung from places of business had increased. ABII came out with a policy for sending dependents home early. They also hinted at substantial cutbacks in the ABII commitment to the Iranian government. It looks like a lot of people will be going home at the beginning of the year, some (mostly dependents) because they want to and some because they have to due to job eliminations. We received a telephone call tonight: "Your president supports the Shah who kills innocent people, so the innocent people are going to kill Americans." An Iranian employee of TCI probably got a hold of an ABII telephone directory and was going down the list. Many of us received the call. In talking to an Air Force Intelligence officer, I found out those threats have never been backed up with action; however, there have been cases of people who had not been called but have had their home or car firebombed. One ABII family who was having a poker party had their house firebombed, but no one was hurt. They moved out of their home into the 21 Complex the next morning. There was no school today, and the power went out from ten this morning to noon.

ABII Security

"Last night at about 8:00 p.m., three Molotov cocktails (firebombs) were thrown over the fence into an ABII apartment complex. One hit the windshield of a company car, breaking the glass, but the bomb did not ignite. Another firebomb was thrown over the fence and rolled in the open area under a building. This one did ignite and caused some property damage; however, no personal injuries were sustained.

The following alert from the American Embassy was received at 1:00 p.m. today:

- Tehran American School will be closed December 7 through January 6, 1979.
- The American Embassy will be closed for normal business on December 10 and 11.
- Americans should display extreme caution from December 7 through 12.
- All Americans, to the extent possible, should remain in their residences on December 10 and11.

Later information from TAS indicates closure until January 6, 1979."[85]

ABII Notice

"Many employees have expressed concern for the safety of their dependents during this month. We are, therefore, offering to furnish transportation to the home location for any dependents now in Iran from today until December 15.

We are now in the process of negotiating a reduction of our contract. The negotiations will result in a substantial reduction of our present work force. This reduction will be finalized by early January. For those employees who are to be returned to their home company and are so notified before January 15, we will not provide for dependent return transportation to Iran. Those employees who will be remaining in Iran can return their dependents to Tehran at ABII expense any time after January."[86]

"Americans in Iran have been warned by the U.S. Embassy that there have been rumors of further violence during the Moslem month of mourning and they should try to stay out of sight.

The Americans were told to stay away from religious gatherings or any places where crowds gather such as bazaars, mosques or universities. The Moslem month of Muharram began Dec. 2 and runs until Dec. 30."[87]

***

Wednesday, December 6, 1978

The BBC said last night was the quietest night in a week, probably because it hailed and rained. There was some talk of the Iranian government drafting all eligible males into the service. I doubt if that's wise because it would put guns in the hands of the very ones who are demonstrating. Perhaps the army feels they would have better control over the people if more Iranians were in the army. The BBC further stated that the Iranian government invited Khomeini back into the country if he agrees to abide by Iranian law. Nora is giving some thought to going home early but wants to see what develops on and after Ashura, which is December 11. She is still working at the Army Staff

College and enjoys it. If she had to give it up, I'm sure she would go home. I called about the availability of ski buses. Despite all that has happened, the buses plan to start operations on December 21.

9:00 p.m.

The electricity stayed on today—the first time in four days. School has been out since December 3 and is not scheduled to open until the sixteenth, if then. We were told today not to come to work on the ninth, so that is five days off, confined inside the house.

ABII Notice

"This is the information phoned to headquarters on December 4, 1978, 4:00p.m. for answering inquiries:

Demonstrations occurring nightly around Tehran with varying intensity. Sporadic gunfire by the military to disperse crowds is evident. None of the demonstrations have been directed toward ABII or its personnel. No ABII personnel have been involved.

American Embassy has confirmed that the following reports are false:

- That the embassy came under attack on December 2.
- That two Americans were killed in Tehran on December 2.

ABII personnel and their families are being instructed to keep a very low profile, including dress conservatively and curtail travel around Tehran as much as possible.

There were two fire bombings December 3 involving residences of one American military and one civilian—no report of injuries.

There were confirmed reports today involving an attack on a police station. This is our first report of opposition using firearms.

TAS school opens as of today until further notice. Community School closed through December 13.

Questions asked by Hadley Road:

Curfew – No change

Mail – Slow, customs still on strike

Are all our people working? – Yes, but not necessarily in previous work location

Taxi service – Normal

Gas situation – Lines have all but disappeared"[88]

<u>ABII Notice</u>

"TCI officials have advised us that Saturday, December 9 [this date was added as a hand note, per my supervisor], Sunday, December 10, have been declared official holidays as well as Monday, December 11. All ABII regular, casual, and contract employee are not to report to work on these days. …

Please keep in mind that the coming week is a period of deep mourning in Iran. Please restrict your activities as much as possible. If you cannot avoid going out, please dress conservatively and avoid any areas where people are gathering.

The last day of class for this semester at TAS is today, December 6. The new semester will begin January 6, 1979."[89]

***

Thursday, December 7, 1978

It rained off and on all day. We shopped at Super Parmis and encountered long lines for food. In the evening, we went to the Griffeses for pizza and got home around eight thirty. The electricity went off again from nine to midnight. Every time the electricity goes off, and we've already gone to bed, we are awakened when the lights come back on. I can never remember when the switch is down if the lights are on or off; it varies from room to room. Once we were up, we lit some candles and listened to *As Time Goes By* and sipped wine.

"Suddenly the lights go out, caused perhaps by yet another sudden strike by electrical workers. Shots are fired in front of the house. The man orders his wife and children to stay away from the window in case firebombs are thrown. And he stands close to his new fire extinguisher hanging on the wall.

Although Americans generally aren't the target of violence in Iran, public feeling against them is growing, and nerve-wracking experiences such as this are increasing fears for their safety. Perhaps 35,000 American workers and their families are continuing to sweat out the violent demonstrations against Shah Mohammad Reza Pahlavi and his military government. But thousands more have left the country and some U.S. companies, Westinghouse Electric and Bechtel among them, are flying out their employees.

Those who remain are victims of fear and tension, often the result of constantly circulating rumors. The U.S. Embassy in Tehran has set up a 24-hour telephone information service in an attempt to calm fears and to squelch the wilder stories. But with the sound of gunfire and shouting breaking the night, even an American baker who lived through the shooting in Beirut, admits, 'I don't even feel safe in my own home.' ...

Americans in Iran will mostly be staying inside, behind locked doors. Many are concerned that the propaganda that has been launched against all foreigners, particularly Americans because of President Carter's support of the shah, might develop into violent anti-Americanism. This propaganda is coming from all of the factions opposed to the shah: the Moslem religious groups, the students, and the growing number of terrorists."[90]

***

Friday, December 8, 1978

It was raining again. Went to church and helped with Communion and the Advent service. Only about half the normal church attendance was there. I talked with some people, and it seemed like most were thinking of leaving. In the afternoon, we walked down to the Saltanatabad Drug Store and purchased a new *Time* magazine. Our part of town appears "normal"; however, there is a large number of army troops walking around.

The BBC says there will be a large demonstration on December 10 at the Shahyad Monument, a demonstration of a million people. We find ourselves and our lives regulated by when the news comes on. NIRT only broadcasts in English three times a day(noon, two, and five), and TV programs are in English only once at six thirty in the evening. Webster had called twice today to confirm/deny rumors he heard and to pass on some new ones. We look forward to his call to break the monotony. I called my parents at 7:45p.m., but the call only lasted five minutes. My parents said the news in the US concerning Iran was bad and wondered if we were going to leave. I told them not yet. Ron Craig called about a rumor concerning military dependents leaving. It's certainly possible, considering ABII flew out 158 dependents the night of December 6, and 150 more on December 7.

After we put the kids to bed, we went down to the Parkers for an "after curfew" drink and listened to the BBC some more.

A Christmas card to my parents:

Where do I start? I guess by saying "for details see Time and Newsweek." Gunfire at night, tanks rolling down the streets, school canceled, gas strikes, no electricity, no mail. But we are still "enjoying" the experience. The company has started offering to fly dependents out, but Nora has not made up her mind. We want to stay together if at all possible. Rumors are wild—the Shah abdicating, civil war—but no one knows for sure. ABII's involvement in Iran has been cut back substantially, so it looks like we may be home by mid-year for good. On the bright side, skiing starts the twenty-first with transportation provided to the slopes. We intend to stop off in Europe on our way home, whenever that is. Here is wishing you a Merry Christmas. Next year, we will probably be there with you. There is no mail going out, so I had Terry Scott hand carry this when he returned to the States for mailing. Love, Us

***

Saturday, December 9, 1978

It rained again, and there was no school or work. Went shopping at Super Parmis while the kids did schoolwork at home. I read, and Nora played the guitar. The Griffeses came over for Mexican food. We shared pictures of our trip to Greece we all took in October and drank some retsina Greek wine.

There are big marches scheduled for tomorrow at the Shahyad Monument and the Mehrabad International Airport, which will be closed for forty-eight hours to all incoming and outgoing flights. We heard that AT&T called the ABII President H. Kertz (who was over here during this problem period) on December 6 and asked him how many planes he needed to get us out. AT&T was all set to charter and send planes to get us. Kertz declined the offer, but word of this kind is encouraging.

Tonight was eerie; there was no noise of any kind. No cars. No chanting. Nothing but complete silence across the whole city. The only exception was the sad classical music that was being played by the BBC.

"The shah ordered tanks into Tehran streets and the airport closed, creating near panic among thousands of foreigners trying to flee Iran. ...

Thousands of frightened foreigners, many weeping, jammed fog-bound Tehran airport in a desperate scramble to flee the country before the expected eruption of new violence."[91]

***

Sunday, December 10, 1978

Woke up early after a fitful sleep, anticipating what today will bring. There is no work or school.

The ABII evacuation warden came by yesterday to confirm where we lived. The plan is for us to go to the TAS Lavazan campus and be airlifted from there to the Mehrabad Airport or Doshan Teppeh Airport if evacuation is necessary.

It was still raining today. We listened to the *Voice of America* this morning, but no news about Iran. The BBC is much better. We spent the day cooped up in our house, cutting out paper Christmas trees and stringing popcorn, hoping we would be here for Christmas. I frequently went to the window, opened it, and listened for chanting or any sound that would indicate a demonstration. Only once in a while I heard some distant chanting.

The NIRT radio news broadcast at noon was twenty minutes late—the first time that's happened since we've been here. At 12:20p.m., Webster called. The word from the embassy was that tanks had formed a straight line from Koursh-e-Kabir Boulevard across the north part of the city to Pahlavi Avenue. Unconfirmed reports say the Shah and his family left the city. Later, we received another call from a friend who had seen the tanks, which were set at block intervals across the city to keep any demonstrators from coming north.

We listened to the BBC news at nine thirty tonight. There were marches over one million strong that stretched over four miles today. Although peaceful and well organized, extensive vandalism was done to the Shahyad Monument with paint. Webster called again. Word from the embassy is there's supposed to be a big march up Saltanatabad Boulevard (just east of us) at midnight.

"Without a single violent incident, hundreds of thousands of Iranians staged their biggest protest march to date against the foundering authority of Shah Mohammad Reza Pahlavi.

The disciplined, well organized march through the capital lasted for more than six hours and lent considerable weight to the religious-dominated opposition's claims to being an alternative government.

The performance was all the more impressive, since by agreement with the government, almost all troops and police were absent from most of the sprawling capital, especially areas hard hit by arsonists and rioters in earlier demonstrations.

Marshals in the street—and turbaned mullahs (clergy) atop buses using hand-held loudspeakers—regularly reminded the crowd to avoid the violence so feared by the organizers.

Although the shah's name was mentioned neither on banners nor in chanted slogans, the whole day was clearly a show of no-confidence in the 59-year-old monarch. ...

Estimates of the numbers of marchers varied from the absurd to the biblical. The government-controlled radio first spoke of only 'tens of thousands,' but later mentioned 'around 400,000' while the National Front opposition claimed about 3 million of the capitals 4.5 million residents took part."[92]

***

Monday, December 11, 1978

We didn't hear any march at midnight. Today was another quiet day in our part of the city. The BBC reported there were marches, and they were not peaceful as both "right" and "left" groups mixed with army soldiers. The next-door neighbors, the Priors, secured the movie *Dove* from the army base and showed it in their home. The kids enjoyed it since it was the first movie, or anything like it, they had seen in four months (TV has been off since the first of December).

The embassy called the Priors to say they're pleased with the results of the demonstrations today; no killing, looting, or burning. TCI is not working tomorrow, but my group is. Our neighbor Rev. Prior, who has been here for the last eighteen years, feels the Shah has already left the country and the military is compromising with the moderate demonstrators, which is very "un-Iranian." He also told us he and his family are giving serious thought to leaving. He stated words to the effect of, "When our family leaves, I want my family on the same plane."

ABII Notice

"This year, the Shia Moslem Holy Day of Ashura falls on December 11. Ashura is the day of deepest mourning for the Moslem people. It commemorates the death of Imam Husain [Husayn ibn Ali]…Traditional mourning in remembrance of the sacrifice of Imam Hossein [Husayn] and his family has included chanting of prayers. Some Moslems beat themselves on the chest with their hands or on their backs with tassel-shaped chains so that they may feel some of the pain felt by Imam Husain [Husayn] and his family.

During the mourning period of Muharram, the American Embassy suggests Americans should show respect for Moslem traditions in the following ways. Make no effort to watch religious ceremonies, and under no conditions bring photographic equipment near a religious ceremony or parade. Loud parties should not be held, and record player and radio volume should be kept low. Women should be discreet in their dress in public (wearing head scarves and avoiding bright colors would be recommended).

The December 9–11 mourning period would be a good time to catch up on family business rather than engaging in significantly visible public and social activities."[93]

"In Tehran, hundreds of thousands of persons streamed through the streets chanting 'Down with the shah!' It was the second mass protest march in two days, and like Sunday's, it ended peacefully. As night fell, the government reasserted its authority, sending tanks and troops back into the center of the city and reinstating a full curfew and ban on demonstrations. …

At the Tehran demonstration, a huge throng massed around the towering, arch-like Shahyad monument—end point of the march and symbol of the shah's rule—was told by opposition leaders, 'We will continue until victory is won!'

The Tehran marchers took over the center of the city, parading down main avenues. …

Anti-American sentiment, stemming from the United States' long-standing support for the shah, was scrawled across countless placards carried by the marchers. 'Criminal Americans Go Home,' read some, or 'Iran Will Become Another Vietnam.'

The giant march followed the same 5 ½-mile route used in the similar procession Sunday. There was no official estimate of size…but it was at least as big as Sunday's—which the official news agency said involved 400,000 people, but observers said amounted to closer to one million."[94]

"An estimated 2 million demonstrators, shaking their fists and beating drums, surged through the streets of Tehran today shouting 'death to the shah' and 'Yankee go home.'…

The Tehran procession, which began as several hundred thousand people marched into the streets chanting religious slogans, swelled as women, elderly people, small children and student leftists joined the parade.

Demonstrators said the crowd was much bigger than Sunday, when 1.5 million people took part in an eight-hour demonstration…

Young girls in ankle-length black veils and youths with dust in their hair—a sign of deep mourning—carried flowing triangular flags in green, the Islamic color, in red for the Moslem martyrs and in black for general mourning for ancient Shiite saints and anti-shah demonstrators killed in recent clashes with the army.

'Victory is close,' many shouted. 'We have Allah's blessings'"[95]

***

Tuesday, December 12, 1978

I went to work today; however, there was no school. One of the Iranians I work with, Mr. Goharinajad, is very happy about the outcome of the marches. He is very anti-Shah. I asked him about Karim Sanjabi's attitude toward Americans (the opposition leader who was released by the Shah on December 7).Mr. Goharinajad told me one of Sanjabi's demands to the Shah is that foreigners are welcomed as equals, whatever that means. It looks like ABII is the backbone of the expatriate community because the military and other companies are looking at the conservative telephone company as to what to do. Rev. Prior mentioned this also. This bothers us a little. We hope the company doesn't try to be a "hero." The embassy is giving little guidance.

Nora did a little shopping today, and I got a haircut. Then, we took the family to the Evin Hotel for dinner, where they had a Christmas tree up with all the trimmings. About60 percent of those eating in the restaurant were ABII employees. On the way home, we dropped off our Christmas cards at Terry Scott's, who was flying home for Christmas. Since there is still a mail strike, that is the only way we can get our cards out. Upon returning home, Claire said my parents called. (We share the same telephone line.) Whatever the papers are printing about everything happening here, it must be bad. I wanted to tell my parents we are all fine and would certainly leave if we felt we were in danger. Unfortunately, the circuits were busy when I tried to make a call back through the switchboard. So I just left my number for the operator to call back if they find any time. They never did.

A new frustrating aspect of this job and location is the boredom. ABII started flying out dependents at company expense December 6.Nora and the kids elected to stick it out with me (Nora said because ski season was about to start).A total of four hundred dependents out of the entire ABII community of about two thousand went home. Another six hundred are on vacation and will be gone until the first of the year.

"The Iranian Government, which means the Iranian monarch of Shah Mohammad Reza Pahlavi, is evidently hanging by a thread. Its stoutest supporter in the world is the American government, and President Carter says he doesn't know if the shah will survive.

The British, who created Iran's vastly profitable oil industry, are beginning to revise their assessments of the shah's chances. Their leading papers suggest that he may have to go. His hold on the throne is growing weaker each day, they say, and despite the backing of an army of more than 200,000 well-equipped troops, despite his being a great patriot, the shah's once imperious control is rapidly dissipating in scenes of bloody riot. Pragmatically as always, the British are looking to their interests, which, they say, lie in the stability of the country and not in the survival of any particular monarch.

We can't agree that the situation has deteriorated beyond the possibility of the shah's recovering control. He controls the army, and the army can control the streets as long as its commanders are steely enough to order their troops to fire into the crowds when necessary.

But there are rumors of desertions and small mutinies, which should not be surprising. The Shah himself, in his heavily guarded palace, is reported to be talking about turning himself into a constitutional monarch."[96]

***

Wednesday, December 13, 1978

I went to work again, but there was no school. After work, I went Christmas shopping with Gordon. The electricity was out from nine o'clock to midnight.

Everything is either on strike or closed down due to the civil unrest. Nora is going crazy trying to stay busy. Even the military college canceled classes this week. That combined with the kids being home is enough to drive her mad. She has, and still is, considering going home; however, the logistics are formidable: renting a furnished apartment, buying a car, getting the kids situated in school, etc. If I knew for sure that I would be going home in the first or second quarter of 1979, it would be a different story. Not knowing means Nora might well have to turn right around and come back in May or June, undoing everything she had done initially. Even the damn snow isn't falling right. It has been raining here and in the mountains for the last week; it's just not cold enough to snow. Nora and I have at least settled on one thing. If and when we get back, we are going to invest what money we have left in a cabin or house by Tahoe, Truckee, etc. The wanderlust in this old kid has abated for the time being. Unless things really pick up around here, I'm coming home as soon as they let me. There is not enough work here to keep me busy all the time, and I feel staying longer would dull my competitive edge (with Pacific Bell). Raj, my old boss, is back in San Francisco for the holidays and is putting in a good word for both of us with Dave Short, an AVP for PacBell. I have written both Short and the new vice pres., Jo Fasciona, just to give them a personalized view of what is happening over here politically and to keep in touch—trying to prevent the old case of "out of sight, out of mind." If Dave can't fit me in, maybe Jo needs a good second-line manager in the operator services department. Actually, I anticipate little trouble with my old department.

Back to Iran. While there were some anti-American slogans, the majority were against the Shah. The main thing Iranians hold against Americans is Carter supporting the Shah. There seems to be little, if any, resentment because we are working to improve their country. Just looking at salary (not benefits), ABII is among the lowest paid of the expatriates. I have no complaints about ABII. Iranians seem to know what we make, and because we are closer to their salary than other expats, it makes for a better working relationship.

***

Thursday, December 14, 1978

I made arrangements for a cab to take the entire family skiing at Dizin. Fantastic! It's the only word I can use to describe the slopes at Dizin, which are open with no trees, and the longest run is four miles! The whole family enjoyed getting out and doing something for a change. It was almost like being home and skiing at Lake Tahoe.

When we were taking our second run, I put Tori and John in a gondola two cars in front of the one we were going in. An Iranian joined us. As we were going up the lift, a gust of wind came up and blew the gondola between the kids and us off the haul cable, sending it crashing down on the mountain and rolling to the bottom. Nora and I were gripped with fear. The Iranian laughed and said, "Not to worry, that happens all the time."He explained the gondola was pressure clamped to the haul cable, so if someone was in it, his or her body weight kept the car attached to the cable. We were not relieved. I looked at the bottom of the ski run, and there were many dented gondolas in a pile. For the rest of the day, all four of us made sure we were all in the same one, putting as much weight in it as possible.

Once we got home, the electricity went out from eight thirty to midnight again.

"Three anti-shah extremists disguised as soldiers raked an army barracks with gunfire…wounding 20 government troops before being killed themselves, official sources reported.

Informed sources in Tehran disputed the official version of the barracks attack. They said it occurred Monday afternoon when an unknown number of Iranian enlisted men burst into an officers' mess and sprayed it with automatic weapons fire. The sources said at least 12 members of the shah's elite Palace Guard were killed and more than 20 wounded.

The sources, who asked not to be identified, could not say what happened to the enlisted men who allegedly killed the officers. It was the first reported attack on officers by enlisted men since religious leaders called on soldiers to stop shooting anti-shah demonstrators."[97]

***

Friday, December 15, 1978

Nora and I put together a decision chart for the repercussions of leaving or staying. It helped us arrive at the decision we made when we found out the schools would be closing after New Year's.

Ken Dyer dropped by for a few beers to talk about what was happening. We invited the Parkers up. Electricity went out again from eight forty to eleven thirty.

ABII Notice

"About 370 dependents of ABII employees in Iran returned to the United States between December 7 and 10. The departures followed a company offer to furnish transportation to dependents who wished to leave Iran during the Moslem holiday of Ashura, during which civil unrest was anticipated."[98]

***

Saturday, December 16, 1978

The kids finally went to school today. The electricity was out again for four hours tonight. We're not sure if the army is doing it or the demonstrators, but we are using a lot of candles! Nora found out tonight that all teaching of the Iranian officers has been canceled. With no more job, she is very disappointed.

***

Sunday, December 17, 1978

The radio and TV are back on. With the mail situation the way it is, we haven't heard from our parents in over a month, except by phone. Hadley Road in New Jersey says they have over six thousand pounds of mail for Tehran that has not been sent due to the conditions over here. So who knows when we will get mail, bills, etc.? I wrote my parents on the thirteenth and sent it through company mail; hopefully, they got it. Still no word on the working situation or who is going where. Each day is a real drag; almost all work has stopped due to the contract renegotiations. But I spent the morning calculating some coefficients for call completion by using multiple regressions.

Through company mail, I received a very nice letter today from Jo Fascione (PacBell VP) advising me of "company happenings" as they relate to people I know. It was very nice of her to take the time.

The kids are back in school until the twentieth. Out of a pre-civil-unrest school population of 329, there are only 89 left; however, there are more than enough teachers! Looks like they will finally get a good education since there's one teacher for every ten students or something like that.

We have our Christmas tree up and decorated with gifts under it (I'm glad my parents gave us their gifts before we left). The house is decorated, and we are all ready for Christmas. Things in Tehran have quieted down for awhile. Most people are waiting for the end of Muharram to see what the Shah does. They are giving him a chance to catch his breath before more protest his governing. Since so many foreigners have left, those remaining are treated very well. We have received excellent service from taxi companies, as an example.

Dear Mom and Dad,

Hi! Happy Anniversary; Merry Christmas; Happy New Year's! And now I'm thirty-four (how ancient). Sorry I haven't written for awhile, but I got tired of describing "low profile," where the tanks were, who shot who, who left when, and what is there to say about five days of no TV, no radio, no newspapers, and no going out? I am sure Ashura was much more exciting over there. It really was dull here, to say the least. We did three jigsaw puzzles, played twelve games of dominoes, twelve games of backgammon, wrote letters for Christmas cards, and talked and talked, but life is looking up.

The skiing is fantastic. We went last Thursday and plan to go again this Thursday. I will also go with the kids on the American Women's Club bus on Sunday. The kids are back in school until the twentieth, and I go back to work on January 2.There are only 89 of 350 students in the kids' school. Good grief, the lights just went on. They were only off two hours tonight. For the last four nights, they have been off for four hours, so we are making progress. I am calling Colonel Sagdican tomorrow about school. Out of eight teachers, there are now two of us left plus one new one, so I don't know what he will want to do. A U.S. Colonel talked to him, and he seemed shocked so many Americans had left. We shall see what happens.

I am making "Barbie clothes" with Claire for Tori, all jeans and T-shirts. It's fun. We are working together on it over morning coffee. I called the U.S. embassy about a rumor, but they can't verify it. The

147

skiing is good. We have a Christmas tree and all our nice Christmas ornaments plus the wedding bird, but I miss the silver bells. I don't wear a scarf, and everyone is still very nice to me. I now get a taxi in five minutes, and they ask if they can come back the next day. I even had the owner of Auto Charlie Taxi drive me last week. What I remember most is the lady in the black chador who told the store owner Claire and I were ahead of her in line. That never happens over here. People usually push and shove to be first. Tomorrow is another general strike, but the black flags are coming down. An ayatollah had a dream that Husayn came and asked why everyone was being so mean to the Shah. Strange as it may seem, this will probably be the reason there will be peace around here for a while anyway. I am reading the book The Shah and getting insight into some of the history behind all of this. It is all very interesting as long as I can ski, work, and the kids stay in school. Now TAS is the only school "not" in session (the kids are at Piruzi). There were articles in Time and Newsweek. I don't know whether we will be coming home in January or not. It all depends on John's job. Let's see, what else can I say? Did you see the Venture fall magazine and see Tori's picture? My new maid is very good and nice. She cooks for us too! Mother, I did not enjoy our last conversation. Take everything you hear with a big grain of salt. Papers love making headlines, and now with no Israel peace signing, oil prices going up, and whatever Carter thinks of next, you won't hear so much about us. Relax!

***

Monday, December 18, 1978

No electricity from eight thirty to eleven tonight.

ABII Notice

"As previously announced, ABII is running buses to the ski areas beginning December 21, 1978.Sight-seeing buses will depart Shah Abbas every Thursday at 9:00 a.m. for Dizin and Ab-Ali and should begin the return trip no later than three. Ski buses will be available for trips to Dizin, Shemshak, and Ab-Ali every Thursday. For the holidays through January 3, ski buses will also run to Dizin on Saturday through Wednesday.

Buses are provided at no expense to the employee and are strictly for the use of ABII employees and family members."[99]

"Iranians observed a day of mourning for more than 1,600 demonstrators killed in the revolt against the shah this year. In general, the capital was calm, but there were violent demonstrations in two key provincial cities. …

Meanwhile, throughout the capital of Tehran, under warm winter sun, most stores stayed closed, including those in the wealthy northern suburbs."[100]

***

Tuesday, December 19, 1978

No electricity from eight thirty to eleven.

ABII Notice

"Hadley Road Information Call – As of 3:15p.m.

Demonstrations have <u>decreased</u> significantly in Iran over the past week. Tehran is extremely quiet. Dissidents called for a day of mourning for Dec. 18.Many shops in Iran were closed. However, essential services were not disrupted. Oil workers have returned to work and production is increasing. But production has not yet returned to normal levels."[101]

ABII Notice

"In observance of Christmas, ABII will close at 12 noon on December 24 and remain closed December 25.

In the interest of coordinating holidays more closely with TCI, ABII will observe a normal workday on New Year's Day, January 1, 1979.When the official Iranian calendar designating holidays for next year is available, the holidays to be observed by ABII will be designated."[102]

"Shah Mohammad Reza Pahlavi has reacted 'positively' to a plan to replace Iran's martial law administration with a 'government of new faces,' to ease tensions, political sources said today.

The sources said the shah had totally rejected an earlier plan by former Prime Minister Ali Amimi under which the monarch would have turned his vast powers over to a crown council.

The sources said Dr. Gholam Hossein Sadighi, imprisoned five times for his political opposition to the shah, would soon take over as prime minister and begin forming a cabinet."[103]

***

Wednesday, December 20, 1978

No electricity again from eight thirty to eleven tonight.

ABII Security

"The situation in Tehran appears to have returned to normal conditions. Information received from the embassy indicates that Americans may now travel throughout the city. Employees and dependents who desire to travel to the south part of Tehran should exercise extreme caution and be alert for demonstrations that could flare up. Most of the bazaar area is now open, and it appears that business is returning to normal."[104]

ABII Notice

"To All ABII Employees and Their Families,

When I had breakfast with many of you at the Tehran Hilton last June, I said that ABII had done a tremendous job in putting the Bell System's best foot forward and showing others, who did not know us, just who we are and how we can perform.

Today, in the spirit of this season, and mindful of the marvelous efforts you have made to date, I reiterate those statements—only with a louder voice. I think you are doing an outstanding job. The results you have achieved convincingly confirm the Bell System's capabilities.

Obviously, no one is absolutely certain at this point about the future course of Iran. But I feel sure that we will continue to serve the country in developing its telecommunications system. And I'm just as certain the future will see the Bell System with broader international involvement, thanks in large measure to what you have done and are doing.

You are eyewitnesses to an eventful time in Iran's history. In the process, you are writing a proud new chapter in the book of significant Bell System accomplishments.

As we enter this holiday season and prepare for the new year, let me assure you that although the miles between us are many, you are very much in our thoughts, and your example is one in which your colleagues throughout the Bell System share great pride.

Sincerely,

John D. deButts

Chairman of the Board"[105]

We also received a letter from Hubert L. Kertz, Managing Director and President of ABII. It was similar in nature, but it did include two paragraphs worth noting:

"A recent example of this coordination was the successful effort to return almost 400 dependents of ABII employees to the United States. It was indeed gratifying to see the tremendous effort put into this endeavor by our staffs in Tehran and at Hadley Road [New Jersey]. I'm not referring to employees just 'doing their jobs.' I'm addressing ABIIers who put in long grueling days—and nights—to ensure that every dependent who wanted to return to the United States could and did.

What lies ahead for ABII in the new year is hard to predict. We know there will be more changes in Iran, and our working relationship with Telecommunication Company of Iran will be adjusted to accommodate these changes. But whatever happens, we will be better prepared to meet any new challenge."[106]

***

Thursday, December 21, 1978

No electricity from eight thirty to eleven. Taking the ski bus, we went skiing again today at Dizin. We feel so lucky to be able to get away from the demonstrations and riots for at least a day.

***

Friday, December 22, 1978

We had a Christmas brunch with the Parkers; about forty people came. To avoid the curfew issue, we held it from one in the afternoon to seven in the evening. Without diversions like this, one could go crazy, thinking about where the next Molotov cocktail will land or if the embassy will give the green light on evacuation. Fortunately, we are well stocked with liquor (thanks to my Air Force Reserve status), so the parties are a great success. The electricity was out again tonight from eight thirty to eleven.

***

Saturday, December 23, 1978

I worked today, but the kids were out of school for Christmas vacation. The electricity was out again in the evening from eight thirty to eleven.

ABII Security

"On Saturday, December 23, 1978, two executives of Texaco Oil Company in Ahwaz were assassinated. One of the individuals was an American and the other, an Iranian. The assassinations occurred shortly after 7:00 a.m. in different sections of Ahwaz as each individual left his residence en route to work. The two executives were ambushed and killed by automatic weapons. Information obtained about these two individuals indicates that they have been very outspoken during the period of social unrest and specifically concerning government employees on strike in the oil fields. It is assumed that they were assassinated because of their involvement in attempting to break the oil strike.

Between the hours of 6:00 and 8:00 p.m. on Friday, December 22, 1978, two propane gas bottles with the valves open were placed in the boiler room of the Western Electric office facility here in Tehran. When the furnace ignited, an explosion occurred causing damage to the basement, first and second floors, and breaking windows in an adjacent building. No one was in the building at the time of the explosion.

With the resumption of the Iranian high schools yesterday, demonstrations occurred throughout the city of Tehran. No violence or destruction of property resulted from these demonstrations.

ABII families are encouraged to observe safety precautions during the next week. It is not known at this time just how far the student demonstrations will go; however, our people are advised to stay out of high school and university areas."[107]

***

Sunday, December 24, 1978

Violent demonstrations started again today. There was shooting and some killing in the south part of the city. As time goes by, the role ABII will play in the development of Iran dwindles. Today, the "brass" is having a meeting to determine which aspects of the Statement of Work will be eliminated and which will be retained. It seems to me that as more meetings are held, the less our role will be. By January 6, we should know what tasks will remain and who will be going home. Rumor has it that 80 percent of the employee body will be impacted.

The family has mixed feelings. Until it was mentioned that the possibility existed for us to return to the States, the kids were content with staying here. Now, it seems like they're ready to go home. Nora and I aren't ready to quit yet. Much depends on the "tax" package ABII offers to returnees. If it is not substantial, we will end up paying about four thousand dollars for the opportunity to work here. The electricity has been going off nightly for the last twelve days between eight thirty and eleven at night just to annoy the populous (but hopefully it stays on tonight, Christmas Eve!).

The first American, who was an oil executive, was killed yesterday in southern Iran. If only this unrest would "rest," we could enjoy the country. I have been here for almost seven months and still have not been to the bazaar. We stick pretty much to the north part of the city. Nora and the kids are skiing today…lucky for them. I had to take some material to the Kakh Street building, so I'm stuck here. We only work half a day today, so I guess I'll do some last-minute Christmas shopping. The mail has been coming in spurts, taking anywhere from twelve to forty-five days to arrive. One thing you can say about this assignment, it is challenging. Rumor says that ABII's next country to work in will be China. Some individuals have already signed up to go whenever something is decided. We can't even consider it at this time because of the lack of schools, but it would be an interesting work environment. There is a little Christmas party over at the Kakh Street building at eleven this morning, so Webster and I are going to go for a few cookies before I head off to shop.

"Troops opened fire on thousands of young demonstrators trying to storm the American embassy, killing at least eight persons, and renewed anti-shah rioting in provincial cities claimed more lives.

Iranian military authorities warned anti-shah demonstrators to keep off the streets of Tehran and other cities hit by renewed clashes with security units in which an estimated 15 persons died...

The warning was aired by the state-run radio after thousands of youths shouting anti-American slogans tried to storm the U.S. embassy and were driven back by Marine guards firing tear gas canisters. ...

The sudden surge of violence came amid a continuing political deadlock caused by widespread opposition to the shah's attempts to form a reconciliation government. ...

The violence erupted a day after American oil man Paul E. Grimm of Wilton, Conn., was ambushed and machine-gunned to death in the southwestern town of Ahvaz. Grimm, 56, was the first American to die in the civil strife now sweeping Iran. ...

Americans living in Tehran said that they were now experiencing a new form of harassment—taped telephone messages warning them to leave Iran within a specified number of days.

The worst violence occurred around the sprawling U.S. embassy compound.

The embassy clash began as 500 high school students gathered at the main gate shouting slogans. They set a diplomat's car ablaze as troops moved in to disperse them. Regrouping on side streets, the demonstrators threw up barricades and then moved in for another attack, their numbers by then swelled to several thousand. ...

At the beginning of the attack on the embassy, troops were unable to get through traffic jams and Marine guards fought the crowds with round after round of tear gas canisters.

Demonstrators tossed scores of bricks into the embassy parking lot, smashing windshields on dozens of mission vehicles. ...

Thwarted in their efforts to get to the American embassy, the students set fire to a half dozen cars and army trucks and then ransacked the offices of the Israeli airline El Al."[108]

***

Monday, December 25, 1978

Christmas Eve last night was memorable. The electricity wasn't shut off at all, the first time in twelve days!

We went to Mass at ten thirty. It was really crowded; most Americans came out from hiding to celebrate Christ's birth. We then went to the Griffeses for dinner. Excellent ham with all the goodies. Left at 8:45 p.m. to make it home before curfew. Nora's parents called later. My parents had given us gifts when we left the States, so we did have some gifts from "Ema and Epa" under the tree. Since we were trying to discard weight when coming over here, we are so glad we kept most of the packages for Christmas. Mom and Dad had planned it so that there were an even number of gifts for John and Tori. Nora got a tote bag, which couldn't have been more appropriate now that we are in ski season. We listened to the BBC then went to bed. Electricity was off at eight twenty.

"Thousands of chanting demonstrators set garbage fires in the streets around the U.S. Embassy in the third day of protests...They fled as troops swept through the area firing submachine guns into the air. ...

No official casualty count was available but hospital sources said at least five demonstrators were killed around Tehran, including two who were chased inside buildings by troops and shot when captured.

Helicopters directed army squads to trouble spots as the protesters, mostly teenagers from Tehran's closed high schools, went on a rampage in the streets...

Automatic weapons fire could be heard throughout the day, mostly around the U.S. Embassy, where troops took a particularly tough stance, firing into the air as they charged groups of students and kicking out their bonfires.

Troops also moved swiftly to disperse about 300 young boys and girls as they marched on the luxurious Intercontinental Hotel shouting slogans against Shah Mohammad Reza Pahlavi and the United States."[109]

***

Tuesday, December 26, 1978

This Christmas was like no other. We were not able to send any gifts to mine or Nora's parents due to the mail problems. So we decided to hand carry them when we return in the next few months, assuming we are doing that. The latest from ABII is "the fat is in the fire," or we've presented our position to TCI; now it's up to them to tell us who stays and who goes. Some individuals have already been told to pack up and go home. Many students were killed yesterday near Tehran University. Nothing is coming from the palace, which is bad. The people are giving the Shah only a few more days to meet their demands. Only God (Allah) knows what will happen.

Dear Mom and Dad,
Merry Christmas! Thanks for the phone call on Christmas morning. We had a very nice Christmas. The kids were very happy and pleased with their toys. I made "Barbie" clothes for Tori's Barbie doll. We got John G.I. Joe, some doll clothes for Joe, and Legos. Today, they have been up since 6:45a.m. It is now ten thirty, and there has been no screaming, so they must be happy. I took them skiing on the twenty-fourth, and we actually had fun with just the three of us (John had to work). They were very good, and Tori is hard to catch now, as she skies

the moguls. She is so fast and daring. I never see John unless he waits for me. I can always spot him, though, as he is the only skier on the hill who jumps as he skis straight down the hill. The kids and I plan to ski on the twenty-seventh, twenty-eighth, thirtieth, first, third, and fourth. We will then pick up John for some skiing on his weekend. No one passes us on the hill now, so I guess we are getting pretty good. As long as we ski, all the problems seem to melt away.

John got me some brass kerosene lanterns for Christmas, but now we need to get some naft (lamp oil), and the line is a block long. I have a nice cab driver who will help for a price. No one uses candles for the atmosphere anymore. We save them for blackouts. The electricity has gone off at 8:15p.m. for twelve days in a row, excluding Christmas Eve. We watched a 1950s movie until midnight and felt we had real luxury. I tried to explain to the kids how Christmas was giving to those less fortunate than us, so we gave Nargas, our maid, a thousand rial note, which is fifteen dollars, and the garbage boy (thirteen years old) one hundred rials and an old toy. He was so delighted that he rang the Parkers' bell and asked for his Christmas present. Oh well, it was a nice thought, right? Nargas gave us the prettiest little Iranian thing; it is brass and is like a saltshaker or something similar. She gave John a nice little dish and Tori a vase with roses. She is so nice and a good worker. I feel, especially in these times, it is important to go out of your way to be nice. Nargas supports herself, three of her own kids, and two from another family. I think I am the only one she works for right now since so many have left.

We have a lot of young student cab drivers now, and the worst thing you can do is be labeled "American khehlee (very) Bad," so we are very nice and fair about everything and have never experienced any trouble. Claire got caught in a demonstration on the twenty-third, and she sat with all three little blonde-haired kids in the cab, smiled, and spoke Farsi; nothing happened. We almost got caught in it too, but we were farther down the street. Because of the problems, the bazaar is closed again and so is the Iranian high school. Education is obviously not a big deal over here. Our kids will start January 6 with hopefully no interruptions. Iranians would never harm children; they love them. We went to a nice church service on Christmas and to the Griffeses for a delicious, sixteen-pound ham dinner until about 8:45 p.m., when we headed home to beat curfew. After dinner, we played the Washington version of dominoes. I looked in every store in northern Tehran for marshmallows for my crème de menthe dessert. I finally had to make them; I used Claire's blue crème de menthe and added food coloring.

I mailed you a letter last week from an Iranian yellow mailbox. Did you get it? We haven't gotten mail for over a week and no Christmas cards. We are planning on buying a rug from Tabriz before we leave. They are very expensive but very beautiful, and I think handmade rugs are almost a lost art in Iran today. I hope my job starts up again; however, there are plenty of jobs around now with people leaving. Claire Parker and I are still very well stocked with everything. I'm getting fat from all this sitting around. Right now, little John feels under the weather, so I suppose we will cancel some of our ski days. Many people have already received their notices to leave, so I don't know how long we will be here. I'm just glad we stayed for Christmas.

THE OUTCOME

Wednesday, December 27, 1978

9:30 a.m.

Time is running out for the current government, as trouble erupted in Tehran again today. There were many killed yesterday by the army, whose presence had been more noticeable throughout the city contrary to a week ago. This morning, tanks and armored personnel carriers roll down Koursh-e-Kabir Boulevard on their way to south and central Tehran. Some people pick up stones and throw them at the tanks. Paper floats down from the upper floors of the TCI buildings in protest to the killings and the presence of the army. Almost all contractor work in the city has stopped. Gas lines are forming again, and most necessities for daily life are in short supply. There are long lines for *naft*, which is cooking oil for the small stores the Iranians have. Also, there's a shortage of heating oil.

11:30 a.m.

Coming to work, I tried to get gas for the company car. I went to three stations; one was closed with a line waiting for it to open, and the other two stations were open with lines waiting for gas to arrive by tanker trucks. The lines were at least a mile long, and the wait was about three hours. I decided not to wait and try again later tonight or first thing in the morning after curfew ends. Oh yes, we still have curfew from nine at night to five in the morning. Nora told me the cleaning woman's daughter was wounded by a stray bullet in the shooting yesterday. And to just "complete" the picture, John is sick today with strep throat. Fortunately, medicine is easily obtainable. Work for ABII is almost at a complete standstill because we're waiting for TCI to tell us which tasks we can continue and which ones have been eliminated.

12:30 p.m.

All hell just broke loose! From our windows, Webster, Tony, and I watch cars coming down Koursh-e-Kabir from the north with their lights on, horns honking, and stickers on their windshields. The employees at TCI continue throwing paper out the windows, some of them even yelling "Allah Akbar!" Now, they are beginning to throw pictures of the royal family out the window; big pictures of the Shah and his family members are dropping from the upper stories and crashing on the driveway mall between the TCI-1 and TCI-2 buildings. I can't find the words to describe what's happening. It's "raining portraits" of the Shah, the Shahbanu Farah, and Prince Reza, hundreds of them sailing down from all the windows of both buildings. Once on the ground, employees are stomping and kicking them. All the Shah strived for over the last few decades is being destroyed. The people want to rule themselves. Traffic is stopped on Koursh-e-Kabir Boulevard because people are just watching as the employees continue to throw pictures, paper, and other objects out the windows.

TCI seems to be a gauge for the political feelings of the populous. As the country goes, so does TCI. It is now 12:45p.m., and things have quieted down for the time being. My boss, Gordon, just called to check on us. From across town, he noticed choppers flying over our section of the city and wanted to make sure things were okay. Including us, there are only twenty-eight Americans in the TCI buildings right now, when it used to be hundreds. Traffic is still at a standstill on the boulevard, but now horns are honking, and drivers are yelling at the people in the buildings, who yell back.

1:00 p.m.

The quad between the two buildings looks as if it had snowed since it's covered with paper, adding-machine tape, shattered pictures of the royal family, and some trash. Troops just arrived; there are five soldiers with M-16s and a sergeant with a .45 caliber pistol. He removes the pistol from the holster, cocks it, and the six of them shoot into our building. A policeman finally runs up, stops them, and starts talking to them. The soldiers walk away and position themselves around the mall between the two buildings, rifles "at the ready." I move back into my office, but I can hear noises down the hall. It sounds like a crowd of people. Suddenly, about twenty employees and demonstrators come into my room, tearing the pictures of the Shah and family off the wall, breaking them up, and throwing them out the window. More soldiers show up and fire shots into the air. This place is turning into a war zone! I call my boss, and he tells us to get out if possible. I tell him we're safer here in the offices than down with the soldiers. They will probably shoot at anything.

1:30 p.m.

A long line of armored personnel carriers is moving down Koursh-e-Kabir, one carrier after another interspersed with a few big Chieftain British tanks on flat beds. I count about twenty or more. Soldiers are marching alongside them. The phone lines to our building have been cut, so no calls are coming in or going out. More and more papers are coming down from the upper floors, car horns are still honking, and traffic has not moved.

It looks like it's going to be a long afternoon.

Just heard another shot. Soldiers have now totally blocked off the street and are spreading up and down Koursh-e-Kabir. The armored personnel carriers have stopped, and some of them have turned into the park between the two TCI towers. I can see soldiers positioned behind the machine guns mounted on top of the vehicles. Bill Koch, executive director, came over from Kakh Street for a meeting and stopped by to see if we were all okay. He had to leave his car blocks away and walk through all the demonstrators as well as the army. Every car in sight is now honking, and paper continues to drop from the windows. Everyone's trying to remain calm during all this. I must admit, we probably look strange sitting here while the TCI employees are going from room to room, looking out windows. Another shot. There are about five people in my room now, throwing paper out the windows. They leave me alone and just take paper out of the trash baskets or off other desks.

2:00 p.m.

There has been rapid fire for the last fifteen minutes on the street just below my window. They must be firing into the air. At least, I *hope* they are firing into the air. I'm having trouble seeing who's shooting because of the window ledge, but I don't want to lean out too far for fear I'd make a nice target. One of the troops just threw a tear-gas canister. Now, more automatic gunfire. The traffic has been diverted from Koursh-e-Kabir. No one can get in or out of the building complex. More shooting. I'm staying right here until all this settles down. The Iranians in the building are friendly; however, one just asked me why President Carter supports the Shah, a difficult question to answer right now. Police and troops are converging on the street below. They have shotguns, machine guns, rifles, and clubs, certainly a formidable force. Another shot. Police are using loudspeakers to try and disperse the people. Bill Koch said there is an embassy alert, but he isn't sure of the content. Still no phones working; no way to tell Nora what's going on. Hope we get out of here okay.

2:30 p.m.

I stepped into the room next to mine at the same time a girl threw some paper out my window .She was shot at. The bullet hit the window ledge, spraying shards of marble into the office. Webster, my coworker, told me it is time to leave. The phone lines are finally working again. I call Nora to tell her not to worry if I'm not home at the usual time. She tells me Steve Parker called and told her the embassy is under siege, cars are burning, and shots are being fired. There is also trouble in the

Takhte Tavoos building. Windows have been broken and cars set on fire. It is past quitting time for TCI employees. Yet, they are still here. I don't know when this is going to end. Semiautomatic gunfire again followed with more shooting. Now, there seems to be a lull. Mr. Goharinajad just brought his lunch in and is eating. I guess for them, this is merely another day. For me, it is the first time I've been shot at or at least close to live fire. I've decided the best way to pass time is by taking notes. The sun finally came out; it's the first time today. Maybe that will help, but I'm probably being optimistic. The only real thing that will help is a change in government with the Shah leaving.

4:00 p.m.

We are finally out of the building. Our normal work hours are 6:45 a.m. to 3:15 p.m., so we aren't delayed much, considering what is happening. On the way out, we took an elevator. After we entered it, the operator changed direction and headed up for some reason. On the thirteenth floor, the elevator got stuck and wouldn't go up or down. We all started banging on the door, and the operator yelled something in Farsi. About twenty minutes later, the maintenance man showed up to unlock a switch so we could manually open the door. What a day!

Once in the lobby, Webster got a company car. As we walked through the lobby, we noticed demonstrators and army soldiers sitting together having tea. After the shock of seeing the two groups together wore off, we continued driving out of the courtyard. The soldiers waved at us. We know we will not be back.

"Iran's political crisis appeared to reach an acute and decisive stage...after a day of wild shooting and lawlessness in the capital and a strike that effectively shut down the oil industry.

Trucks and cars burned in Tehran streets, soldiers opened fire with automatic weapons on a funeral procession after they reportedly shot their own colonel, and the city became a bellowing sound stage of sirens, gunfire and car horns.

Tear gas, smoke from pyres set aflame by anti-shah demonstrators, power cuts, stores shutting and merchants piling their stock on the backs of trucks—Tehran almost visibly tottered and with it the peacock throne of Shah Mohammad Reza Pahlavi. All schools were closed and the state air, rail, and bus services were not functioning. ...

Karim Sanjabi, the leader of the National Front, the main opposition political body, renewed its call during the day for the shah's abdication. Members of the group said that they believe that the time was at hand when the Carter administration might want to drop its support for the monarch, since he appears increasingly unable to control the population, or Iran's oil, the essential factor in the country's geopolitical position."[110]

"Troops opened fire on demonstrators today as oil production plunged to a 27-year low, halting exports for the second consecutive day. Iran radio announced gasoline rationing.

Witnesses and opposition sources said at least eight persons, including three soldiers, were killed in a clash between troops and mourners around Tehran University.

The witnesses said tens of thousands of students, professors, clergymen and doctors had joined the funeral procession for a 27-year-old civil engineering student killed Tuesday.

Troops attempted to halt the procession as it neared the university and when mourners refused to disperse the army opened fire, witnesses said.

'There are ambulances all over the place,' one American witness said. 'There's blood all over the streets and people running with blood dripping from their hands.'

Opposition sources said the shooting started when troops tried to take the young professor's body from the ambulance-hearse in which it was being carried."[111]

***

Thursday, December 28, 1978

Steve Parker and I got up at four thirty this morning to leave the house by five to get gas for the cars. The BBC said there was going to be gas rationing today, and we wanted to get a jump on the crowds. It took us five minutes to get to the gas station, but the line was already a mile long. After a two-hour wait, we were finally able to fill up. The Iranian idea of gas rationing was to operate only half the pumps, but when you finally get to one, they fill you all the way up. No ski buses today due to the gas problem.

It's Nora's birthday, so the Parkers, Nora, and I went out to dinner at Hugo's, located in the Tehran Hilton. For the four of us (the kids stayed home), it cost $175, but the diversion was worth it—what a dinner. Besides the four of us, there was one other table with people in a restaurant that could hold about two hundred. Strolling between the two tables were three Iranian musicians playing background music. When approaching our table, we explained it was Nora's birthday, and they asked what we would like to hear. Steve said, "I Left My Heart in San Francisco."They sang it well with an Iranian accent. It was a tearjerker, knowing that was probably our last dinner together in a country we loved with the people we loved. It was so memorable, a huge room with only two tables occupied and silence interspersed with quiet conversations and a few songs.

It was around that time we heard no American airlines were permitted to fly to Iran anymore. It might be they were not allowed to land, but it wasn't clear. The only way in and out was on "foreign" airlines. AT&T in New York and our managing director and president of ABII, Hubie Kertz, are working with foreign airlines to take the families out of Iran and home to the U.S. if it becomes necessary.

***

Friday, December 29, 1978

Tori was sick with a temperature of 101.Since Nora had things under control, the Parkers, son John, and I went skiing for probably the last time. With the gas problems and the threat of evacuation, we might never be back. It was a beautiful day, great skiing, and no crowds. They were probably all in Tehran waiting in gas lines.

The electricity went out at night, as usual, but John and I still went to church at six. There were only nine people there, including Fr. Williams. On the way home, I turned onto a street demonstration where people were yelling and burning tires. I told John it was a street repair crew, but I don't think he believed me. Even with the windows up, John and I were both coughing and gagging in the car from the smell of burning rubber. But I was afraid to open the windows because the demonstrators had surrounded the car. I was trying to determine what to do, when an Iranian banged on the driver's side window and yelled in English, "Follow me!" He yelled something in Farsi to the crowd, and they let him guide me to a side street. All of a sudden, it was almost quiet. The smell of burning rubber dissipated, and the demonstration continued to move down the street I had just left. There was no sign of our "savior"; although, we were fortunate he had helped us. The street we were on was absolutely quiet as we drove home.

Letter written by Nora's parents to us dated today was sent back to them with the stamp "Service Temporarily Discontinued; Return to Sender."

Dear Doolittles,

It was nice to get the call this morning. It was the worst connection we've had. We were hoping to hear from you, and you were coming home, but we keep telling ourselves you have proved quite capable of taking care of yourselves. We just finished calling John's parents. They had called us after not reaching you on your birthday. Today, we heard the Shah is not abdicating but leaving the country for awhile. The military is out, and there will be a Crown Council with an opposition Prime Minister Dr. Shahpour Bakhtiar. No one knows just what that might mean. Today, a mysterious Iran airplane landed near Washington, DC, and there were rumors it carried the Shah's mother and other family members. We have also heard we have one of our aircraft carriers (Constellation) on the way from the Philippines.

Love, Mom and Dad

"The political situation unraveled further here...as a flood of confusing, sometimes contradictory, rumors spread quickly through the capital.

Efforts to form a new civilian government appeared to be continuing, leading to reports that Dr. Shahpour Bakhtiar, the deputy leader of the opposition National Front party, had been named head of the new government and that Shah Mohammad Reza Pahlavi had agreed to leave the country temporarily. …

Also, there were reports early in the day from Washington that at first were taken to mean that a U.S. naval aircraft carrier force was headed toward the Indian Ocean, either as a show of force or to aid in evacuating Americans here.

However, an official U.S. spokesman said later that a carrier and its escorts had been ordered to leave their base in the Philippines and to cruise into the South China sea but that the ships had not been sent to the Indian ocean."[112]

***

Saturday, December 30, 1978

7:30 a.m.

Today, I'm at work. None of us know anything about what will happen and when. I spent most of last night trying to convince Nora to leave; things are only going to get worse. She promised she would think about it. My work has come to a complete stop. We are not even receiving any intercompany mail because no one wants to come to this building. Mr. Goharinajad told me there's going to be demonstrations today, so I called Gordon and told him that at the first sign of trouble, Webster, George, Narvos (one of the other ABII employees), and I were leaving by company car. No taxis, buses, or company transportation are running due to the gas shortage. I've heard that within the next few days, the bakeries will not have enough gas for their ovens, which means no bread, which means the majority of the poor people will have no food. Not a good situation. To complete the picture, there is no garbage pickup, so all the trash is stacking up in the streets.

10:00 a.m.

We all left TCI due to the demonstrations. After taking George Tears home, I went down to the Shah Abbas building to get traveler's checks and rials. I was home by noon. Nora and I went to the tennis club to see if we could get any of our dues back. It was closed, and Mr. Vesi, the owner, had left the country. All that was left in the club was a huge chandelier hanging from the ceiling.

3:00 p.m.

It is the beginning of the end, perhaps my last day at work. Once I got home, I decided to go through my stuff and throw out what I didn't need any more, like the large box of business cards that had my name on the front with my senior engineer title, etc., and on the back was the same thing in Farsi. I took about twenty-five to keep and threw the rest away.

This evening, I received an interesting phone call, one of many, from a neighbor asking when I was going to install their phone. Some were calling from homes as far away as a mile. All the calls were conducted in English, albeit sometimes slow and careful. I asked them why they thought I was going to install their phone. They told me they received my business card in their yard. When I asked them where they lived, they said on the cross street just outside our cul-de-sac. Apologizing for the mistake, I politely told them I was not in the installation business. In piecing the incident together, I decided some teenager or adult retrieved the business cards from the trash and tossed them over fences as he or she walked down the street. A little humor in a somewhat melancholy day.

***

Sunday, December 31, 1978

No work today. Piruzi School, where John and Tori go, is not going to reopen after the holidays on January 6. So we started gathering our things and did an inventory. The Griffeses had a New Year's Eve party, and we attended, along with the Parkers, Greeks, Hillards, and others. During the party, there were numerous embassy alerts strongly recommending dependents go home, and some of the guests got calls saying the Tehran American School was not going to open for six months. Work was also postponed indefinitely. The party ended at eight (due to curfew), so we all sang "Auld Lang Syne" in a circle, wished each other a Happy New Year, and left. All of us knew there was a very good chance this was the end. The mothers had already decided that without school, they were going home. Most of the dads knew that without the wives and families, the work would not continue. Parker and I dropped one of our cars off at work.

"Soldiers loyal to Shah Mohammad Reza Pahlavi killed hundreds of Iranians...in retaliation for the murder of seven military and police officers, witnesses and opposition leaders reported.

Three of the officers, belonging to the SAVAK secret police, were tried in a 'people's court' set up by a frenzied mob in Mashhad and hanged Saturday. Others, including an army colonel, were killed in different incidents Saturday, witnesses said. ...

On the political front, the official radio reported the resignation of Prime Minister Gholam Reza Azhari; the shah accepted the resignation and asked Azhari to stay on until another cabinet is formed.

The shah had already asked Dr. Shahpur Bakhtiar, a liberal opposition figure, to form a government to succeed the Azhari's military administration."[113]

"Shah Mohammad Reza Pahlavi will leave Iran 'for a while for the purpose of medical treatment and relaxation' for the second time in his 38-year reign, his government announced early Sunday.

The 59-year-old shah's decision came at the end of crisis talks Saturday with the elders of Iran's parliament and opposition leader Shahpour Bakhtiar, whom he named premier to succeed Gen. Gholam Reza Azhari. ...

Highly placed sources, however, said the shah would leave only after the new civilian government was comfortably settled 'probably before the Iranian weekend (Friday)'...

The announcement climaxed a year of nationwide protests and bloodletting that has plunged Iran into chaos."[114]

"The U.S. Embassy in Tehran has advised American dependents to leave Iran in the face of continued violent

opposition to the shah's government, the State Department
announced…

The recommendation to leave the country, at least
temporarily, was directed to dependents of American officials
and military personnel and to families of American civilian
workers.

'In view of the scarcity of heating oil, gasoline and kerosene
in this winter period, and in light of the conditions prevailing in
the major cities of Iran, the embassy recommends that
dependents of American citizens temporarily leave the country,'
the State Department said.

State Department spokesman Tom Reston said, 'This is not
an evacuation, this is a voluntary action.'

Asked what prompted the action, Reston said 'I think the
embassy has been monitoring the situation closely and just
decided in light of the events in Tehran, it was appropriate at this
time.'"[115]

***

Monday, January 1, 1979

Today, we heard the embassy is "recommending" all Americans
leave. They can't do more than that; if they ordered us to leave, they
would be responsible for getting us out. We spent hours thinking about
what that meant. The schools are not starting in 1979, so most of the
wives and mothers want to head back to the US. The ABII employees,
on the other hand, think the unrest will finally end and work would
resume. But it does not look promising.

The air controllers walked off the job at seven thirty this morning.
Only two flights got off; neither one was for ABII. So now we just wait
for some word on when and how to leave. There is no gas to fuel the
buses to take people to the airport, so it looks like we are fortunate to
have a car. The town is dead. Shops are closed. Gas stations are closed.
Very few people are on the streets. The air controllers' demands include
one that states, "American planes be forbidden to land because President
Carter supports the Shah." The AT&T chairman of the board was
supposed to arrive today. It looks like AT&T is considering pulling us all

out. We listened to NIRT and the BBC all day. Just heard the airport is now open, and American planes are coming in.

My boss called and said TCI will be closed for up to two weeks, company vehicles are not to be driven, and the employees who are out of the country must stay out. If and when we send our dependents to the US, they will be on company expenses (forty dollars a day). The chairman of the board never made it to Tehran; he stopped in Paris. I just got a call that the airport is still closed. So much for the BBC.

My parents also called. I decided, with their input, to send the family home. Then I called Shah Abbas, the company admin headquarters, and told them. Nora and I spent hours deciding what to take home and what to leave. There was no guarantee anything we shipped would arrive, but the time spent packing helped keep our minds off what was going on in the city. Even John and Tori were deciding what to take home. ABII gave us boxes, and we packed what we didn't need on a day-to-day basis. At night, we listened to the BBC, our only news from outside of Iran.

The electricity continues to be out every night from eight to eleven.

"Hundreds of Americans and other foreigners fled Iran's upheaval in U.S. Air Force transports and commercial airliners today while more anti-Shah demonstrators fell under the gunfire of soldiers. ...

Strikes by airport workers turned Tehran airport into chaos and disrupted commercial flights. Some of the Americans were flown out on U.S. Air Force transport planes, including the huge C-5-A Galaxy, the plane that was used to fly evacuees from Vietnam in 1975.

The Defense Department in Washington said 85 U.S. government dependents left Tehran late Monday night on an Air Force C-5 and another 75 were flown out later on a C-141 transport. It said three such flights a day were scheduled, taking out government dependents first and non-official Americans later if commercial airliners cannot fly in.

Diplomatic sources in Tehran said there were 4,200 Americans in Iran who want to leave this week. There were about 40,000 in the country before the trouble started but about 10,000 already have left."[116]

***

Tuesday, January 2, 1979

Nora, John, and Tori finished packing and got ready to leave. We decided what to ship home and what to leave, what they'll take with them on the flight and what they won't take. We checked the bags two or three times to make sure they had what everyone needed. During the day, I got a call saying the family was leaving tomorrow, as were the Parker dependents. Steve Parker and I took their cat to the vet to get some kind of tranquilizer so the cat could fly home with Claire and the family on the plane. As the doctor gave the cat a shot, he defecated all over Steve, which was perfect since Steve never did like the cat. I found out later that when Claire landed in New York, she let the cat out to "stretch its legs." It dashed off instead, never to be seen again.

"With new waves of violence engulfing Iran, many more Americans and other foreigners fled the country by plane…Conditions were so chaotic at Tehran airport that Iranian Air Force fighter planes intercepted two charter flights and forced them to return to Tehran.

Iranian soldiers moved into the air control tower and replaced striking air controllers, leading many panicky refugees to decide to stay in Iran until flying is safer.

Demonstrators demanding the overthrow of Shah Mohammad Reza Pahlavi fought running gun-battles with soldiers in the streets of Tehran. Witnesses said three persons were shot to death by soldiers. …

Scenes at Tehran airport were frantic throughout the morning…with hundreds of persons trying to flee the country. Pan American said two of its 747s landed there…despite the air controller strike and flew refugees to London and to New York. …

A U.S. State Department official said in Washington that in view of these two incidents one U.S. military plane was sent into Tehran to find out if U.S. flights would be forced down. The plane was not impeded and other flights were sent in."[117]

***

Wednesday, January 3, 1979

Nora and the kids are evacuated, flying with KLM Airlines. The plane was five hours late getting off.

Memo to Self,

We got up this morning at three and got Tori and John ready for our trip home. We were picked up by a small van at the house at four, met others at the Shah Abbas building, and got in a big bus to make the trip with everyone else to Mehrabad Airport. Looking out the window, I saw lines of Iranians waiting to get gas for cooking, which went on for miles. People were also standing around fires in empty metal drums.

We took off on a KLM 747 for Amsterdam after a six-hour wait at the airport. We were sitting on our coats playing bridge on the floor with kids running all over. We landed in Medina, Saudi Arabia to get more fuel because there wasn't enough for a longer flight. Upon takeoff, we all heard a loud thump and felt it. I knew something was wrong when the steward (they were all men) came by the emergency exit, saw Amy Parker sitting there with her two dachshunds and a cat, and said, "Oh shit." The pilot came on the loudspeaker and told us with everything we had been through in Tehran, he was going to tell us everything that was happening. He wasn't sure, but he thought we had lost a wheel or two, and the landing was going to be difficult. He then gave us a briefing on how to land in the "crash" position. The air temp was twenty-four degrees outside in Amsterdam, and if we overshot the runway, we would land in the sea. I looked around, and it was all women, children, and animals. We had all been up since three.

The Stevensons were across from me. Claire had dark circles under her eyes, and her two little girls were occupied with books and dolls. Claire's daughter Amy was in front of me. The pilot told us everything he was thinking and worrying about. All of a sudden, the most important thing was do I sit between John and Tori, or do I sit by the window, so I can push them out in the aisle if I need to? The pilot told us to put everything of value in our pockets (passports and cash) and pray we make it. When we approached Amsterdam, we did a fly-by at the tower, and the pilot was told we had lost two wheels. When everyone was told to get into the crash position, my Hiatal hernia forced me to stand up to clear the problem in my chest. People started yelling at me to sit down. They thought I was having a heart attack. I finally was able to sit down in a crash position. We finally landed safely. The runway was covered with foam, and there were fire trucks and ambulances all around. It was freezing when we got off the plane. We had to walk down the steps to reach the ground. I tried to get Tori to put on her coat, and all she would say was "no." I finally gave her to an airport employee, and she finally got her to put her coat on. We are all fine now, in a good hotel, with a nice dinner with the Stevensons. The Parkers and the Griffeses took other planes from the airport to other destinations. Another "little" Iranian adventure.

The flight from Amsterdam to the States was somewhat uneventful. Tori had an earache and was crying as we lifted off. The stewardess knew what to do, put a hot compress in a cup and told me to hold it over Tori's ear. It immediately helped relieve the pressure, and Tori fell asleep. When we got to Chicago with three sets of skis, poles, and boots, and three huge bags of "stuff," we proceeded to customs. The woman in front of me was the first one from our evacuation flight. The customs agent asked what she had to declare. She leaned over the counter and said, "Honey, I have everything of value I could jam in the suitcase." He didn't look up, just asked where she was traveling from. She straightened up a little and with a degree of pride said, "Tehran, Iran." He took his stamp, stamped her passport, and said, "Welcome home. Next."

He never looked up but just kept stamping our passports one after another. A large porter came up to me and said, "Ma'am, you look like you need some help." I thanked him, tipped him generously, and he helped us get to our next flight.

"Parliament today approved formation of a civilian government to replace the tough military regime imposed by Shah Mohammad Reza Pahlavi on a citizenry bent on topping him from his peacock throne.

Installation of the new government could pave the way for the shah's departure from Iran on an extended vacation that could mitigate the violent struggle to dethrone him.

Some diplomatic sources went further, saying that such a 'vacation' could well turn out to be a permanent one that would spell the end of the shah's 38-year reign."[118]

***

Thursday, January 4, 1979

Shapour Bakhtiar is the new prime minister, replacing Gholam Reza Azhari, who lasted fifty-nine days. I continued packing our household goods and ate dinner with Steve Parker at Ken Corricello's home. Went home but couldn't sleep. Woke up at two thirty in the morning.

***

Friday, January 5, 1979

I finished packing. I found out the wives and kids made it to Amsterdam. The plane had to make an emergency landing because it lost two of its tires on takeoff. Hugh Campbell, Steve, and I had dinner at our place—canned stew I had purchased from the commissary. I was trying to finish off as much food, beer, and liquor as possible since we had accumulated quite a stash over the months of shopping. Talk centered on our families and what was going to happen to us and the ABII project.

***

Saturday, January 6, 1979

I repacked everything to "hide" a few mementos to take back with me, like the American flag, which had been flying most of the time in our backyard since the Fourth of July. I also wanted a few of Nora's paintings she had done of the local people, as well as some of the liquor that had been saved. Ken and I walked around town taking pictures. Later on, Gordon joined Steve, Ken, and I for dinner at our home; I was still trying to clean out the pantry.

After a two-month strike, the *Kayhan International* paper was available again.

"Prime Minister Shahpour Bakhtiar…presented to the Shah a Cabinet lacking both the stains of association with the period of repression and, his critics contend, a wide base of popular support.

Bakhtiar has been expelled from the National Front, and religious leader Ayatollah Ruhollah Khomeini, who recent events have shown has de facto veto power over political decisions in Iran, has called his government 'illegal.'

About the mission of his Cabinet, Bakhtiar said, 'The Shah will reign and we will rule'. …

The prime minister declared he would try to lead Iran toward social democracy. He has promised a gradual end to martial law, complete freedom of the press, freedom of political activities and association, and a relentless stand against separatists.

Outlawed political groups would be allowed to operate freely if they proved loyal to Iran and unbound to foreign powers, he said.

Bakhtiar is said to believe in the separation of church and state. But he has repeatedly declared that respect for Islam would be one of the guiding principles of his premiership.

He said…he hoped Ayatollah Khomeini would 'honor' us by returning to Iran. He has blasted French newspapers for attributing to him insulting statements about Khomeini."[119]

"Exiled Shiite Muslim leader Ayatollah Khomeini…praised the major Iranian newspapers for successfully leading a strike against press censorship and called on their staffs to resume work.

'I thank the newspapers' staff who refused to obey dictatorial censorship,' the Ayatollah said, 'and now that a new illegal government has claimed to have lifted censorship the press workers should end the strike and continue production until our account is squared with that illegal government.'…

Khomeini branded Shahpour Bakhtiar's new government 'illegal' and called for 'a day of national mourning' on Monday. But Khomeini stopped short of demanding the Bakhtiar government's overthrow. A communiqué from his villa in suburban Paris left it to 'the people to decide the fate of this illegal government.'"[120]

***

Sunday, January 7, 1979

Slept. Stores were closed due to a general strike. Nora called from California; they are home.

"Iran's new civilian government encountered serious problems...and its first 24 hours produced no sign of an end to political and economic strife.

In downtown Tehran and in the northern suburbs of the capital, troops fired on roving bands of demonstrators who set fire to piles of tires and refuse and built barricades across key streets. At least one demonstrator was reported killed and more than a score injured by rifle and machine gun fire. ...

Saturday night's statement by Ayatollah Ruhollah Khomeini, the exiled Moslem leader, describing the government of Prime Minister Shahpour Bakhtiar as a creature of Satan and calling on the populace to continue 'the struggle,' was a harsh blow to Bakhtiar. ...

With large numbers of troops, reinforced by blue-uniformed air force units, patrolling the main business district, the atmosphere in Tehran was tenser than it has been for a week. In outlying areas troops smashed windows bearing pictures of Khomeini, and clashed with persons who tried to stop them.

The violence followed four days of relative calm, which came while Bakhtiar was attempting to form a government."[121]

***

Monday, January 8, 1979

Went to Shah Abbas about a partial shipment. However, nothing was confirmed. I ate dinner at Ken's home; we had chili. We heard many were killed today throughout Iran. Ayatollah Khomeini is exerting his influence over the population, asking them to strike and observe days of mourning for those killed by the Shah's forces.

"In Tehran a military officer shot a 10-year-old boy and soldiers firing automatic weapons killed at least five demonstrators today.

Witnesses said the officer pulled out his revolver and shot the boy during a march by several thousand demonstrators in the downtown Pich-e-Shemiran quarter. ...

Three bodies with gunshot wounds were brought into Ferouzabadi Hospital in Rey, south Tehran. An estimated 15 others admitted to the hospital also had bullet injuries.

An unspecified number of wounded were taken to three other hospitals in downtown Tehran."[122]

"The capital witnessed another day of bloody demonstrations. Several cities too witnessed similar scenes. Demonstrators in Tehran hanged two Afghan men accused of stealing. ...

Troops shot dead at least five Tehran demonstrators in the second consecutive day of violence in defiance of the new government formed by Premier Shahpour Bakhtiar. An undetermined number of wounded were taken to three hospitals in the city. ...

Meanwhile, the exodus of American and other foreigners from the country continued."[123]

"In north Tehran it was reported that a crowd of people scrambled on to the roof of a mosque and lobbed hand grenades into the home of an army colonel.

By far the biggest demonstrations was held in the Behesht Zahra cemetery in south Tehran when an estimated 15,000 people turned up to mourn the riot victims killed since national unrest began several months ago. "[124]

***

Tuesday, January 9, 1979

It snowed today, and I spent most of the day shoveling snow and reading. As I sat on the deck under the overhang, every so often, I would stare at the pool through the falling snow and think of what had happened since our arrival. A lot of what happened, I believe, is the fault of the United States thinking democracy is right for every country. As we know from our roots in 1776, a democratic form of government has to come from the bottom up. You can't impose a democracy on people, especially a country where the cultures are so different. The U.S. is so young compared to Iran, yet we feel we know what's better for them. President Carter should have done more homework before pushing the Shah to give more power to the people in such a short period of time.

I cooked dinner for Steve and Ken; there is still food in the pantry.

"Malek-Abhari, managing director of the Telecommunications Centre, has resigned, informed sources said."[125]

"In what appears to be a major turning point, the U.S. Government has advised the Shah to leave Iran while urging military leaders to support the new civilian government in its efforts to achieve a constitutional political settlement. …

This was a 'turning point for the Carter administration which for many weeks had resisted suggestions that it urge the Shah to go,' the [New York] Times commented.

The shift in the official American position has been seen by local observers as a major gain for the new Prime Minister's efforts to open an orderly path to the creation of representative, democratic government in the nation."[126]

***

Wednesday, January 10, 1979

It snowed all night, and I'm almost out of heating oil. But I still decided to have a get-together. In attendance were Steve, Ken, and seven others. I fixed spaghetti. At the end of the night, what was left of the spaghetti was sticking to the walls, where it had been thrown. We are experiencing two electric blackouts a day now.

"Prime Minister Shahpour Bakhtiar was quoted…as saying that Iran faces the danger of a military coup, but that he still expects the shah to leave the country.

In an interview with French journalists, broadcast by Radio Iran, Bakhtiar said 'the shah's departure has been agreed on. It's not important whether he leaves today or tomorrow.'

The prime minister said that although there was a danger of a coup, he didn't think the army would act against national interests and try to stop the shah. 'The shah can't be stopped if he wants to leave,' he added."[127]

***

Thursday, January 11, 1979

The company has decided it's time for me to leave and go home. I cashed in my empty Coke cases at the little store down the street (we paid a deposit on them). We were advised to hand carry anything we really valued because baggage and household goods left behind may not be shipped out. I ate dinner with Steve.

"Prime Minister Shahpour Bakhtiar presented his new government to the Iranian Parliament yesterday, promising free elections and spelling out his foreign policy.

The 63-year-old Bakhtiar said that Iran will not ship oil to South Africa or to Israel, a nation that gets 60 percent of its crude from this Moslem country.

The move against Israel is a show of support for the Arab position in the Middle East conflict. Iran 'has always shown its unity with the Arab brothers and has always supported the rights of the Palestinian people,' Bakhtiar said. Iranians are Moslem, but not Arab.

Bakhtiar told the Majlis (the lower house of Parliament) that he will foster closer relations with Islamic countries, particularly nearby Arab nations.

And he promised Iran's full support for Palestinian 'national independence.'

The new premier also said a nine-member Regency Council will be formed 'by Saturday or Sunday' but did not say when the shah will leave Iran."[128]

***

Friday, January 12, 1979

The sun was out today. For the third time, I was notified I had been rebooked on a flight. Steve, Ken, and Gordon came over to play Risk, and I fixed us all meatloaf. The blackouts continue, so I have to time the cooking just right.

***

Saturday, January 13, 1979

I shopped at Shah Abbas for a suitcase. For dinner, Steve and I had pizza and tamales. I'm starting to run out of the pantry food. There is a tug-of-war between Bakhtiar and Khomeini. Bakhtiar is associated with the Shah, so it will be an uphill fight for power.

ABII Notice

"As hundreds of ABIIers head back to the States, they take with them a part of our hearts. We have not known them long in time, but our common experience has brought us together in close relationships, which we will always cherish in our memories. We will eventually forget the disappointments and hardships and remember only the successes and pleasures. All those who have shared this experience realize how closely our lives have been entwined. As we all ultimately scatter to different states, the ties between us will stretch and hold us together with the strongest of bonds—friendship. For all of the deliverables, this has been the greatest and most valuable. Khoda Hafez—for now."[129]

"Several hundred thousand people packed the streets and grounds of the University of Tehran in a massive opposition show of strength against the regime as the country's major universities reopened after nearly four months.

Apart from one or two military helicopters hovering overhead, no traces of military were to be found around the university campus, which up to a few days ago looked like a heavily-guarded fortress.

Soldiers who had been guarding the campus since it was closed after five students were killed there last November 4, left the area two hours before crowds poured in. They moved two blocks away.

The government of Shahpour Bakhtiar had already agreed to the reopening of Tehran University in response to a call by the National Organization of Iranian Universities. ...

National Front leader Karim Sanjabi and prominent religious leader Ayatollah Taleghani led the crowds at Tehran University and addressed them amidst chants of 'Allah Akbar' (God is Great).

Sanjabi told an audience that after 25 years of imperialism and autocracy, 'we are witnessing the victory in this struggle. This victory is due to the perseverance of the people who did not give up although thousands were martyred.' ...

His dedication to Ayatollah Khomeini became abundantly clear one more time when he told the crowd that the masses or Iran have no other leader than Khomeini. ...

Some banks, shops and businesses in Tehran reopened...Streets which had been empty and deserted for days were again suddenly clogged with bumper-to-bumper traffic."[130]

"Ayatollah Ruhollah Khomeini says he will be the strong man of the new Iranian Islamic republic.

Khomeini told interviewers, 'the Shah will be gone in a few days.' He said that in the meantime Iranians should guard against a military coup by the Shah."[131]

"Prime Minister Shahpour Bakhtiar said he would not succeed in his mission without the support of the majority of Iranians. …

He said his government was determined to bring about a situation in which Iran would be run by Iranians."[132]

"Workers of the Telecommunications Company of Iran will resume work after a two-week compulsory strike, heeding the call of Ayatollahs Khomeini and Teleghani.

A TCI employee said…that in view of the vital nature of their work, they had decided to return, particularly since the religious leaders had approved the move.

He said they had been forced to go on strike by officials of the telecommunications company who had prevented them from entering the building."[133]

***

Sunday, January 14, 1979

I ate dinner with Gordon. The apartment was quiet and lonely. During the day, there were shadows in the rooms that reminded me of Nora, John, and Tori. I miss them a lot.

"Martial law soldiers in Tehran…signaled a dramatic change in the country's political climate when they flaunted pictures of Ayatollah Khomeini, voluntarily stuck red carnations in their rifles and at several places joined the thousands of demonstrators who took to the streets for the second straight day.

There were festive scenes on Shahreza Avenue several times…when demonstrators shouting anti-regime slogans greeted soldiers posted at street corners with sala'ams, bear hugs and kisses. …

At one point, the demonstrators carried several soldiers on their shoulders from the Saadi-Shahreza crossing to Pool-e-Chubi. The soldiers could not help but join in the slogan shouting and waved to onlookers. By and large, the troops remained content by greeting the crowds back and resuming their posts. ...

Tens of thousands of people took to the streets, singing, marching, or just milling around discussing the political situation unhindered by friendly, laughing troops."[134]

"In Tehran thousands of demonstrators surged through the streets while parliament debated Premier Shahpur Bakhitar's rescue program for the troubled nation. ...

The exodus of foreigners from Iran appeared to have increased with strong rumors that the shah's imminent departure in the next few days would bring army reprisals against his opponents and even lead to a military takeover.

Premier Bakhitar, however, repeated his denial that any such move is being considered by the army. ...

Shah Mohammad Reza Pahlavi ordered the country's powerful army generals to back Bakhtiar and stop any attempts at a military coup after the shah's imminent departure from Iran, newspapers said.

The 59-year-old shah paved the way for his departure and the probable end of his reign in the next few days by agreeing on the composition of the Regency Council to help rule in his absence. The nine-member council was officially announced Saturday. ...

That vote of confidence and establishment of the Regency Council were the last constitutional instruments necessary for the shah's long-awaited departure from Iran, also expected within the next few days.

But Bakhtiar, appointed by the monarch earlier this month, still faced his most serious challenge: Iran's exiled religious leader Ayatollah Ruhollah Khomeini, the spiritual guide of the current anti-shah movement, announced in Paris he intends to become the power behind a new Iranian Islamic republic.

While Bakhtiar is often dismissed by opposition elements as a 'stooge' of the shah, Khomeini is revered through Iran. He has already denounced the new government as part of a 'dangerous plot designed by the treasonous shah.'

His new challenge to Bakhtiar's leadership could touch off massive new political turmoil even if the shah quits, and possibly cause the feared military coup by hard-line generals."[135]

***

Monday, January 15, 1979

Woke up at 1:03 a.m. because shots were fired near our apartment. Steve Parker, who helped with my sanity during these last two weeks, left for home today. Also, I found out I was cut from all ABII roles in Iran. Ken and I had dinner with eight taxi drivers at an excellent lamb chelo kebab café.

"General Karim Abbas Qarabaghi, appointed army Chief of Staff last week, said...there will be no military coup in Iran after the Shah leaves the country.

Speaking at a press conference, he however hinted that an army mutiny could not be ruled out. He did not elaborate on this."[136]

***

Tuesday, January 16, 1979

I was picked up early in the morning just as the day was starting, so it was probably around five thirty. There were a number of us on the bus with our bags. We drove through the darkened streets in silence. Every so often, I would see a thirty-gallon barrel with a fire in it surrounded by three to five people trying to keep warm. There was snow on the mountains, so it was cold outside. After numerous stops, we arrived at the Mehrabad Airport at eight. Getting off the bus, we headed into the terminal.

ABII had our departure well organized. The terminal was packed with people, but Iranian ABII employees helped us get ticketed and to customs. After waiting in line for some time, I finally got to the customs agent. He asked me where I was going. I said San Francisco. His response was "good"; although, I don't know if he was happy that I was going to San Francisco or happy I was leaving Iran. I saw the Shah's 707 airplane depart (many pointed his plane out to me). I'm not sure if it was when we arrived at the airport or after I passed through customs. The rest of the day is a blur. I finally boarded Air Iberia for my trip home via Madrid, Spain. The plane took off at two. As it lifted off, I looked out at the landscape. It was the same dry-looking brown landscape I had seen less than a year ago when we first arrived.

In departing Iran and heading for home, I couldn't help but think of a poem I had read in high school by Percy Shelley, "Ozymandias":

I met a traveler from an antique land
Who said: Two vast and trunkless legs of stone
Stand in the desert. Near them, on the sand,
Half sunk, a shattered visage lies, whose frown
And wrinkled lip and sneer of cold command
Tell that its sculptor well those passions read
Which yet survive, stamped on these lifeless things,
The hand that mocked them and the heart that fed;
And on the pedestal these words appear;
"My name is Ozymandias, king of kings:
Look on my works, ye Mighty, and despair!"
Nothing besides remains. Round the decay
Of that colossal wreck, boundless and bare,
The lone and level sands stretch far away.[137]

Once I landed in my temporary destination, Madrid, I heard an American had been killed in Tehran.

"Shah Mohammad Reza Pahlavi, rejected by his people and defeated by 14 months of violence that brought his country close to anarchy, flew weeping to Egypt today en route to the United States and probable permanent exile. Mobs danced with joy in the streets."[138]

Neither the Shah nor I would return.

EPILOGUE

We reestablished ourselves in Pleasant Hill, California. The lady who had rented our home while we were in Iran moved to another location, and the friends who had taken our dog gave us the dog back. I got a new job with Pacific Bell. The kids went back to the same school. With so much catching up to do, we hardly had time to think about Iran or even follow-up with how the country was doing or how our ABII friends were adjusting. After a month, life returned to "pre-Iran." It was almost like the trip had never happened.

Shortly before Christmas, I received a package in the mail. Inside was my small pipe, a tin of Iranian tobacco, and a letter from Webster J. Van De Mark, friend and writer-director. It was the last I heard from him. I wrote him several times, but received nothing in return.

"Ten more days till Christmas in 1979
Dear Nora and John,
It was just about a year ago that we looked out the windows of the seventh floor of TCI for the last time. Actually, it was the twenty-

seventh of December that was the last day of work in TCI, the beginning of the end for ABII.

As you recall, there was a super demonstration at TCI that day. Pictures of the Shah and his family were thrown out of both buildings; troops blocked off Koursh-e-Kabir and occupied the courtyard; periodic shots from small arms, as well as machine-gun fire, could be heard. From then on, it was all downhill for Iran and ABII. Demonstrations intensified in Tehran and the provinces. Severe gas and heating oil shortages made the coming days something that I will not forget for a long while. And if I do, my copious notes on the doings of ABII families living luxuriously in the city will make good reading.

It was the evening after the TCI building had been sacked and secured by troops and the front gates locked with a huge chain that Tony and I decided to get back into the building to take out whatever we could from our offices. It was an exciting venture to say the least. Nothing to compare with a couple of my earlier exploits with the Marines in old 'double-U double-U Roman numeral eye-eye' [WWII], but there were a few tense moments getting in and out. Of course, that is another story you may read in my book.

We packed whatever we could into a small box we salvaged from the rubble. And being the great guy that I am, and at considerable risk to my wonderful body, I went into your office, John, to see if there were any things of value you might have left in our hasty departure earlier that afternoon. I found the valuables I have enclosed. I am sure that you had thought you would never see these things again. Perhaps, by this time, had forgotten they existed.

Anyway, this is my Christmas gift to you both. At this time of the year, when *even* I become slightly mellow, I want to wish you both a very Merry Christmas and the best New Year's yet. And when it's all quiet at night, and after a glass or two of your favorite, listen. In the quiet, and in the distance, you might still hear the chanting from the rooftops…in Iran.

W"

خداحافظ

Khoda Hafez

Goodbye

Above: A view of northern Tehran with the Alborz mountains in the background. Dizin Ski Resort is on the back side of these mountains.

Below: A local sheep herder with his flock one street over from where we lived.

Left: The Doolittle family at a local park northeast of Tehran; the author, son John, Tori, and Nora.

Below: The Doolittle and Parker kids; Leslie Parker, Amy Parker, Tori Doolittle, Frank Parker, and John Doolittle.

Left: December 27, 1978; armored personnel carriers arriving at my work location (TCI 2 building).

Below: Dirt Go USA; this was stenciled on the side of a building in downtown Tehran as a protest against the United States.

APPENDIX

1 February 1979
San Francisco, CA

H.L. Kertz, President
American Bell International Inc.
P.O. Box 5000
South Plainfield, New Jersey 07080

Dear Mr. Kertz:

I would like to express my thanks to you and the people in personnel and transportation for the smooth and professional manner in which my family and I were "evacuated" from Iran. Those involved at Hadley Road and Shah Abbas should be commended. Considering the circumstances, the in-processing for the dependents flight of 3 January and the employee flight of 16 January was extremely well handled. Those of us who were part of the departing mass were awed by the organization and dedication of the employees coordinating our departure. Once back in the U.S., the efforts expended by Hadley Road in job placement and relocation were outstanding. This type of performance exemplifies the familiar phrase "One Bell System...It Works".

While my tenure with ABII was short (7 months), I can honestly say it was the most rewarding and most interesting of my Bell career. I hope that in the future I will have the opportunity to be considered for another overseas assignment and once again be associated with ABII.

Sincerely,

John B. Doolittle

GLOSSARY

ABII: American Bell International Inc.
Allah Akbar: God is Great
AP: Associated Press
Baji: Maid
BBC: British Broadcasting Company
Crown Prince Reza: Oldest son of the Shah and Shahbanu
Dizin: Large ski area north of Tehran in the Alborz mountains
Gholam Reza Azhari: Prime Minister of Iran, November 6, 1978–
   January 4, 1979
Jafar Sharif-Emami: Prime Minister of Iran, August 27, 1978–
   November 6, 1978
Jamshid Amouzegar: Prime Minister of Iran, August 7, 1977–August
   27, 1978
Koocheh: Street
Koochek: Small
MAAG: Military Assistance Advisory Group
Majlis: An assembly of community leaders
Mullah: Local religious leader
NIOC: National Iran Oil Company
NIRT: National Iranian Radio and Television
Piruzi: International grade school in Tehran
SAVAK: Shah's secret service
Shahanshah: His Royal Majesty Mohammad Reza Pahlavi
Shahbanu: Wife of the Shah; Farah Diba Pahlavi
Shapour Bakhtiar: Prime Minister of Iran, January 4, 1979–February
   11, 1979
TAS: Tehran American School
TCI: Telecommunication Company of Iran
UP: United Press
UPI: United Press International

Notes

1. Associated Press, "Peaceful Iran Protest Breaks Six-Month Cycle of Violence," *Washington Post*, June 18, 1978, A20, ProQuest.

2. Bob and Margaret Hauser to ABII employees, memorandum, June 17, 1978, in *Dear ABII*, no.104, June 1978, 2.

3. To ABII employees, memorandum, July 1, 1978, in *Dear ABII*, no. 106, July1978, 2.

4. Nicholas Gage, "U.S.-Iran Links Still Strong," *New York Times*, July 9, 1978, 1.

5. Reuters, "Carter Said to Approve Huge Arms Sale to Iran," *New York Times*, July 16, 1978, 26.

6. United Press International, "65 Safe in Iran Airliner Crash," *New York Times*, July 28, 1978, 4.

7. United Press International, "Iran Reports Outbreak of Cholera in Desert Town and at Gulf Port," *New York Times*, July 30, 1978, 11.

8. Reuters, "Iran Confirms Casualties of Anti-Government Riots," *New York Times*, August 2, 1978, 6.

9. Reuters, "Shah Stresses Commitment to Political Freedom," *New York Times*, August 6, 1978, 5.

10. To ABII employees, memorandum, August 6, 1978, in *Dear ABII*, no. 111, August1978, 2.

11. United Press International, "Iranian Army Seizes Town Hit by Riots," *Press Democrat* (Santa Rosa, CA), August 11, 1978, 7.

12. News Services, "Iran Clamps Curfew on Isfahan after Rioting against Shah," *Washington Post*, August 12, 1978, A15, ProQuest.

13. "Around the World, 10 Americans Injured in Iranian Blast," *Washington Post*, August 15, 1978, A8, ProQuest.

14. "Holocaust," *Kayhan International* (Tehran, Iran), August 21, 1978, 1.

15. "A Mass Murder by Fire," *Time*, August 28, 1978, 28.

16. United Press International, "Ten Arrested in Fire Attack on Iran Theater," *Press Democrat*(Santa Rosa, CA), August 21, 1978, 1.

17. Jerry Wallace to ABII employees, memorandum, August20, 1978.

18. "Great Terror Is Here," *Kayhan International* (Tehran, Iran), August 22, 1978, 1.

19. "Wild Scenes at Mass Funeral," *Kayhan International* (Tehran, Iran), August 23, 1978, 1.

20. To ABII employees, memorandum, August 19, 1978, in *Dear ABII*, no. 113, August 1978, 2.

21. J.L. Shumaker to ABII employees, memorandum, August 29, 1978.

22. "Martial Law," *Kayhan International* (Tehran, Iran), September 9, 1978, 1.

23. J.L. Shumaker to ABII employees, memorandum, September 9, 1978.

24. Hubert L. Kertz, *ABII Bulletin*, (Tehran, Iran: ABII, September 10, 1978).

25. United Press International, "Iran Army Using Restraint-U.S," *Kayhan International* (Tehran, Iran), September 11, 1978, 1.

26. Employee and Community Relations, *ABII Bulletin*, (Tehran, Iran: ABII, September 12, 1978).

27. "Government under Fire in Majlis for Martial Law," *Kayhan International* (Tehran, Iran), September 13, 1978, 1.

28. "Premier's Response Today before Vote," *Kayhan International* (Tehran, Iran), September 16, 1978, 1.

29. Employee and Community Relations, *ABII Bulletin*, (Tehran, Iran: ABII, September 17, 1978).

30. "Majlis Okays Martial Law," *Kayhan International* (Tehran, Iran), September 18, 1978, 1.

31. "Strong 'quakes Rocks Kavir," *Kayhan International* (Tehran, Iran), September 17, 1978, 1.

32. "The Shah's Divided Land," *Time*, September 18, 1978, 32.

33. "NIOC, Bank Strikes End," *Kayhan International* (Tehran, Iran), October 4, 1978, 1.

34. "Strikes for More Pay Spread," *Kayhan International* (Tehran, Iran), October 7, 1978, 5.

35. "Wave of Strikes, Protests Spread," *Kayhan International* (Tehran, Iran), October 9, 1978, 1.

36. United Press International, "Toll Mounts in Iran Riots," *Press Democrat* (Santa Rosa, CA), October 9, 1978, A4.

37. "Three 'Premiers' in a Day!" *Kayhan International* (Tehran, Iran), October 11, 1978, 1.

38. Times Wire Services, "Iran Journalists Strike; 3 Anti-Shah Protesters Killed," *Los Angeles Times*, October 12, 1978, 18.

39. "Army Wins the Day in Tehran," *Kayhan International* (Tehran, Iran), October 17, 1978, 1.

40. "Petrol Panic Brings Traffic to Standstill," *Kayhan International* (Tehran, Iran), October 23, 1978, 2.

41. Buff McWilliams, *ABII Bulletin*, (Tehran, Iran: ABII, October 24, 1978).

42. Jerry Wallace to ABII employees, memorandum, October 24, 1978.

43. "Massive Marches on, off Campus in Tehran," *Kayhan International* (Tehran, Iran), October 25, 1978, 1.

44. Jerry Wallace to ABII employees, memorandum, October25, 1978.

45. Amir Ali Afshar, "Near Clash of Rival Student Protesters," *Kayhan International* (Tehran, Iran), October 26, 1978, 1.

46. United Press International, "Shah Frees 1,200 Prisoners," *Press Democrat* (Santa Rosa, CA), October 25, 1978, A5.

47. "Troops Break Up Tehran Rallies," *Kayhan International* (Tehran, Iran), October 28, 1978, 1.

48. Joe Alex Morris Jr., "11 Killed as Iran Demonstrations Continue," *Los Angeles Times*, October 28, 1978, 3.

49. Jerry Wallace, "Security Update," in *ABII Bulletin*, (Tehran, Iran: ABII, October 28, 1978).

50. Jerry Wallace, "Security Update," in *ABII Bulletin*, (Tehran, Iran: ABII, October 29, 1978).

51. "Student Defiance in Tehran," *Kayhan International* (Tehran, Iran), October 29, 1978, 1.

52. Joe Alex Morris Jr., "Unrest Turns Tehran's Clogged Streets into Chaos," *Los Angeles Times*, October 29, 1978, 17.

53. "Tehran Clashes Leave Trail of Destruction," *Kayhan International* (Tehran, Iran), October 30, 1978, 1.

54. "Three Killed as Rival Protesters Clash," *Kayhan International* (Tehran, Iran), October 31, 1978, 3.

55. Jerry Wallace, "Security Update," in *ABII Bulletin*, (Tehran, Iran: ABII, November 4, 1978).

56. "All Political Prisoners to Be Freed," *Tehran Journal*, November 2, 1978, 1.

57. "Students, Troops in Clash at University," *Kayhan International* (Tehran, Iran), November 4, 1978, 1.

58. New York Friday Cables, "Human Rights Policy behind Unrest-Kissinger," *Kayhan International* (Tehran, Iran), November 4, 1978, 1.

59. Agence France-Presse (Paris), "Khomeini Warns 'Don't Compromise,'" *Kayhan International* (Tehran, Iran), November 4, 1978, 1.

60. C.J. Amendola to all ABII employees, November 4, 1978.

61. Kayhan Reporters, "Bloody Riots Erupt after Troops Open Fire at Tehran University," *Kayhan International* (Tehran, Iran), November 5, 1978, 1.

62. United Press International, "Iran Troops Kill Five in Rioting," *Press Democrat* (Santa Rosa, CA), November 5, 1978, 35.

63. "Two-Month Tale of Destruction," *Kayhan International* (Tehran, Iran), January 7, 1978, 3.

64. Jonathan Kandell, "Iran Premier Quits; Rioters Challenge Army Rule by Shah," *New York Times*, November 6, 1978, 18.

65. Ronald Koven, "Exile Urges Iran Military to Oust Shah," *San Francisco Chronicle*, November 7, 1978, 1.

66. Associated Press, "Iranian Regime Arrests 35 Ex-Officials," *Los Angeles Times*, November 8, 1978, 6.

67. Associated Press, "The Shah's Troops Arrest a Former Premier of Iran," *San Francisco Chronicle*, November 9, 1978, 25.

68. United Press International, "Shah Wins Battle of Streets," *Press Democrat* (Santa Rosa, CA), November 13, 1978, A6.

69. Jerry Wallace, "Security Update," in *ABII Bulletin*, (Tehran, Iran: ABII, November 14, 1978).

70. Walter E. Bartlett to ABII employees, memorandum, November 18, 1978, in *Dear ABII*, no. 125, November 1978, 1.

71. New York Times, "Shah Frees 200 Prisoners, Promises Free Elections," *San Francisco Chronicle*, November 20, 1978, 17.

72. Jerry Wallace, "Security Update," in *ABII Bulletin*, (Tehran, Iran: ABII, November 21, 1978).

73. Walter E. Bartlett to ABII employees, memorandum, November 21, 1978.

74. United Press, "Wildcat Power Strike in Tehran," *San Francisco Chronicle*, November 22, 1978, 15.

75. J.L. Shumaker to ABII employees, memorandum, November 22, 1978.

76. United Press, "Iran Troops Fire on Protesters—Warning of Oil Field Sabotage," *San Francisco Chronicle*, November 23, 1978, 52.

77. Diana Kerry, "Re: Weekend Rumor Control," (Tehran, Iran, November 29, 1978).

78. Jerry Wallace, "Security Update," in *ABII Bulletin*,(Tehran, Iran: ABII, November 28, 1978).

79. "To All Employees," Called to Hadley Road in *ABII Bulletin*, (Tehran, Iran: ABII, December 2, 1978); this was information from ABII HQ in the U.S. to those working in Iran.

80. United Press, "Iran Battles a Mob—Bloodiest Clash Yet," *San Francisco Chronicle*, December 2, 1978, 1.

81. "To All Employees," Called to Hadley Road in *ABII Bulletin*, (Tehran, Iran: ABII, December 2, 1978); this was information from ABII HQ in the U.S. to those working in Iran.

82. United Press International, "Demonstrators Try to Storm U.S. Embassy," *Press Democrat*(Santa Rosa, CA),December 3, 1978, 16.

83. Walter E. Bartlett to ABII employees and families, December 3, 1978.

84. Associated Press, "Gunfire and Tear Gas on Iran's Streets," *San Francisco Chronicle*, December 4, 1978, 1.

85. Jerry Wallace, "Security Update," in *ABII Bulletin*, (Tehran, Iran: ABII, December 5, 1978).

86. Walter E. Bartlett to ABII employees, memorandum, December 5, 1978.

87. United Press International, "Americans Told, 'Stay out of Sight,'" *Press Democrat* (Santa Rosa, CA),December 5, 1978, 4.

88. Employee Relations, "To All Employees," in *ABII Bulletin*, (Tehran, Iran: ABII, December 6, 1978).

89. Employee Relations, "To All Employees," in *ABII Bulletin*, (Tehran, Iran: ABII, December 6, 1978).

90. Bill Paul, "Americans in Iran Sweat Out Violence, Wait for the Next Plane," *Wall Street Journal*, December 8, 1978, 1.

91. Examiner News Services, "29 Killed by Iranian Army on Eve of Holy Days," *San Francisco Examiner*, December 10, 1978, A24.

92. Washington Post, "The March on Tehran: Biggest Anti-Shah Protest Yet," *San Francisco Chronicle*, December 11, 1978, 1.

93. To ABII employees, memorandum, December 9, 1978, in *Dear ABII*, no. 128, December 1978, 2.

94. Associated Press, "Bloody Clash Ends Iran's Two-Day Peace," *San Francisco Chronicle*, December 12, 1978, 1.

95. United Press International, "2 Million Marchers Defy Shah," *Press Democrat* (Santa Rosa, CA), December 11, 1978, A4.

96. "Shah Hanging by a Thread," editorial, *San Francisco Chronicle*, December 12, 1978, 48.

97. Associated Press, "Bold Raid Kills Iranian Officers," *San Francisco Chronicle*, December 15, 1978, 27.

98. American Bell International Inc., "ABII Dependents Arrive Safely at New York," *International Courier* (London), December 15, 1978, 1.

99. Buff McWilliams to ABII employees, memorandum, December 18, 1978.

100. New York Times, "A Day of Mourning in Iran," *San Francisco Chronicle*, December 19, 1978, 11.

101. Employee Relations, "To All Employees," in *ABII Bulletin*, (Tehran, Iran: ABII, December 19, 1978).

102. J.L. Shumaker to ABII employees, memorandum, December 19, 1978.

103. United Press International, "Shah 'Open' to New Government," *Press Democrat* (Santa Rosa, CA), December 19, 1978, A3.

104. Jerry Wallace, "Security Update," in *ABII Bulletin,*(Tehran, Iran: ABII, December 20, 1978).

105. John D. deButts to ABII employees and their families, n.d.; this letter is undated. However, given the subject matter, I placed it in the December 20, 1978, timeframe.

106. Hubert L. Kertz to ABII employees, n.d.; this letter is undated. However, given the subject matter, I placed it in the December 20, 1978, timeframe near the deButts letter.

107. Jerry Wallace, "Security Update," in *ABII Bulletin,* (Tehran, Iran: ABII, December 23, 1978).

108. United Press, "Huge Iran Mob Tries to Sack U.S. Embassy," *San Francisco Chronicle*, December 25, 1978, 1.

109. United Press, "Violent Protests in Tehran, Provinces," *San Francisco Chronicle*, December 26, 1978, 12.

110. New York Times, "Iran Nearly Paralyzed as the Crisis Deepens," *San Francisco Chronicle*, December 28, 1978, 1.

111. United Press International, "Violence Halts Iran Exports," *Press Democrat* (Santa Rosa, CA), December 27, 1978, A6.

112. Los Angeles Times, "New Political Turmoil—Shah Denies He'll Go," *San Francisco Chronicle*, December 30, 1978, 1.

113. United Press and Associated Press, "Hundreds Reported Slain by Iran Army," *San Francisco Chronicle*, January 1, 1979, 1.

114. United Press International, "Shah Soon to Leave Iran," *Press Democrat* (Santa Rosa, CA), December 31, 1978, 1.

115. United Press, "U.S. Families Advised to Leave Iran," *San Francisco Chronicle*, January 1, 1979, 9.

116. United Press International, "Americans Try to Flee Iran: Gunfire in Streets," *Press Democrat* (Santa Rosa, CA), January 2, 1979, 1.

117. United Press and Associated Press, "More Yanks Flee Violence in Iran," *San Francisco Chronicle*, January 3, 1979, 8.

118. United Press International, "Iran Violence Continues as Civilian Government OK'd," *Press Democrat* (Santa Rosa, CA), January 3, 1979, 1.

119. "On the Road to Democracy," *Kayhan International* (Tehran, Iran), January 7, 1979, 1.

120. "Well Done Says Khomeini," *Kayhan International* (Tehran, Iran), January 7, 1979, 1.

121. New York Times, "Iran Strife Continues—New Rioting," *San Francisco Chronicle*, January 8, 1979, 1.

122. "Mourning Violence," *Kayhan International* (Tehran, Iran), January 9, 1978, 1.

123. "Tabriz in Flames," *Tehran Journal*, January 9, 1979, 1.

124. "Violent Protests Continue," *Tehran Journal*, January 9, 1979, 4.

125. "Director Resigns," *Kayhan International* (Tehran, Iran), January 10, 1979, 1.

126. "U.S. 'Advises Shah to Leave the Country,'" *Kayhan International* (Tehran, Iran), January 10, 1979, 1.

127. United Press &Associated Press, "New Iran Leader Fears Army Coup," *San Francisco Chronicle*, January 11, 1979, 18.

128. Los Angeles Times, "Iran's Premier Plans to Cut Oil to Israel," *San Francisco Chronicle*, January 12, 1979, 16.

129. To ABII employees, memorandum, January 13, 1979, in *Dear ABII*, no. 132, January 1979, 1.

130. "Mammoth Opposition Show as Universities Reopen," *Kayhan International* (Tehran, Iran), January 14, 1979, 1.

131. "Khomeini Ready to Set Up Islamic Regime," *Kayhan International* (Tehran, Iran), January 14, 1979, 1.

132. "Bakhtiar Pleads for Nation's Support," *Kayhan International* (Tehran, Iran), January 14, 1979, 1.

133. "Communications and Coal Workers Return to Work," *Kayhan International* (Tehran, Iran), January 14, 1979, 2.

134. "Grinning Troops Greet Street Demonstrators," *Kayhan International* (Tehran, Iran), January 15, 1979, 1.

135. United Press &Associated Press, "New Protests in Iran—6 Cadets Die," *San Francisco Chronicle*, January 15, 1979, 1.

136. "Qarabaghi Rules Out Army Coup," *Tehran Journal*, January 16, 1979, 1.

137. Percy Shelley, "Ozymandias" in *Poems That Live Forever*, ed. Hazel Felleman (New York, NY: Doubleday, 1965), 436.

138. United Press International, "Weeping Shah Heads for Exile in U.S.," *Press Democrat* (Santa Rosa, CA), January 16, 1979, 1.

Bibliography

Afshar, Amir Ali. "Near Clash of Rival Student Protesters." *Kayhan International* (Tehran, Iran), October 26, 1978.

Agence France-Presse (Paris). "Khomeini Warns 'Don't Compromise.'" *Kayhan International* (Tehran, Iran), November 4, 1978.

"All Political Prisoners to Be Freed." *Tehran Journal*, November 2, 1978.

American Bell International Inc. "ABII Dependents Arrive Safely at New York." *International Courier* (London), December 15, 1978.

"Army Wins the Day in Tehran." *Kayhan International* (Tehran, Iran), October 17, 1978.

"Around the World, 10 Americans Injured in Iranian Blast." *Washington Post*, August 15, 1978. ProQuest.

Associated Press. "Bloody Clash Ends Iran's Two-Day Peace." *San Francisco Chronicle*, December 12, 1978.

Associated Press. "Bold Raid Kills Iranian Officers." *San Francisco Chronicle*, December 15, 1978.

Associated Press. "Gunfire and Tear Gas on Iran's Streets." *San Francisco Chronicle*, December 4, 1978.

Associated Press. "Iranian Regime Arrests 35 Ex-Officials." *Los Angeles Times*, November 8, 1978.

Associated Press. "Peaceful Iran Protest Breaks Six-Month Cycle of Violence." *Washington Post*, June 18, 1978. ProQuest.

Associated Press. "The Shah's Troops Arrest a Former Premier of Iran." *San Francisco Chronicle*, November 9, 1978.

"Bakhtiar Pleads for Nation's Support." *Kayhan International* (Tehran, Iran), January 14, 1979.

"Communications and Coal Workers Return to Work." *Kayhan International* (Tehran, Iran), January 14, 1979.

Dear ABII, no. 104, June 17, 1978.

Dear ABII, no. 106, July 1978.

Dear ABII, no. 112, August 1978.

Dear ABII, no. 113, August 1978.

Dear ABII, no. 125, November 1978.

Dear ABII, no. 128, December 1978.

Dear ABII, no. 132, January 1979.

"Director Resigns." *Kayhan International* (Tehran, Iran), January 10, 1979.

Employee and Community Relations. *ABII Bulletin*. Tehran, Iran: ABII, September 12, 1978.

Employee and Community Relations. *ABII Bulletin*. Tehran, Iran: ABII, September 17, 1978.

Employee Relations. *ABII Bulletin*. Tehran, Iran: ABII, December 6, 1978.

Employee Relations. *ABII Bulletin*. Tehran, Iran: ABII, December 19, 1978.

Employee Relations. *ABII Bulletin*. Tehran, Iran: ABII, n.d.

Examiner News Service. "29 Killed by Iranian Army on Eve of Holy Days." *San Francisco Examiner*, December 10, 1978.

Gage, Nicholas. "U.S.-Iran Links Still Strong."*New York Times*, July 9, 1978.

"Government under Fire in Majlis for Martial Law." *Kayhan International* (Tehran, Iran), September 13, 1978.

"Great Terror Is Here." *Kayhan International* (Tehran, Iran), August 22, 1978.

"Grinning Troops Greet Street Demonstrators." *Kayhan International* (Tehran, Iran), January 15, 1979.

"Holocaust." *Kayhan International* (Tehran, Iran), August 21, 1978.

Kandell, Jonathan. "Iran Premier Quits; Rioters Challenge Army Rule by Shah." *New York Times*, November 6, 1978.

Kayhan Reporters. "Bloody Riots Erupt after Troops Open Fire at Tehran University." *Kayhan International* (Tehran, Iran), November 5, 1978.

Kerry, Diana. "Re: Weekend Rumor Control."Tehran, Iran, November 29, 1978.

Kertz, Hubert L. *ABII Bulletin*. Tehran, Iran: ABII, September 10, 1978.

"Khomeini Ready to Set Up Islamic Regime." *Kayhan International* (Tehran, Iran), January 14, 1979.

Koven, Ronald. "Exile Urges Iran Military to Oust Shah." *San Francisco Chronicle*, November 7, 1978.

Los Angeles Times. "Iran's Premier Plans to Cut Oil to Israel." *San Francisco Chronicle*, January 12, 1979.

Los Angeles Times. "New Political Turmoil—Shah Denies He'll Go." *San Francisco Chronicle*, December 30, 1978.

"Majlis Okays Martial Law." *Kayhan International* (Tehran, Iran), September 18, 1978.

"Mammoth Opposition Show as Universities Reopen." *Kayhan International* (Tehran, Iran), January 14, 1979.

"Martial Law." *Kayhan International* (Tehran, Iran), September 9, 1978.

"Massive Marches on, off Campus in Tehran." *Kayhan International* (Tehran, Iran), October 25, 1978.

"A Mass Murder by Fire." *Time*, August 28, 1978.

McWilliams, Buff. *ABII Bulletin*. Tehran, Iran: ABII, October 24, 1978.

Morris, Joe Alex, Jr. "11 Killed as Iran Demonstrations Continue."*Los Angeles Times*, October 28, 1978.

Morris, Joe Alex, Jr. "Unrest Turns Tehran's Clogged Streets into Chaos." *Los Angeles Times*, October 29, 1978.

"Mourning Violence." *Kayhan International* (Tehran, Iran), January 9, 1978.

News Services. "Iran Clamps Curfew on Isfahan after Rioting against Shah." *Washington Post*, August 12, 1978. ProQuest.

New York Friday Cables. "Human Rights Policy behind Unrest-Kissinger." *Kayhan International* (Tehran, Iran), November 4, 1978.

New York Times. "A Day of Mourning in Iran." *San Francisco Chronicle*, December 19, 1978.

New York Times. "Iran Nearly Paralyzed as the Crisis Deepens." *San Francisco Chronicle*, December 28, 1978.

New York Times. "Iran Strife Continues—New Rioting." *San Francisco Chronicle*, January 8, 1979.

New York Times. "Shah Frees 200 Prisoners, Promises Free Elections." *San Francisco Chronicle*, November 20, 1978.

"NIOC, Bank Strikes End." *Kayhan International* (Tehran, Iran), October 4, 1978.

"On the Road to Democracy." *Kayhan International* (Tehran, Iran), January 7, 1979.

Paul, Bill. "Americans in Iran Sweat Out Violence, Wait for the Next Plane." *Wall Street Journal*, December 8, 1978.

"Petrol Panic Brings Traffic to Standstill." *Kayhan International* (Tehran, Iran), October 23, 1978.

"Premier's Response Today Before Vote." *Kayhan International* (Tehran, Iran), September 16, 1978.

"Qarabaghi Rules Out Army Coup." *Tehran Journal*, January 16, 1979.

Reuters. "Carter Said to Approve Huge Arms Sale to Iran." *New York Times*, July 16, 1978.

Reuters. "Iran Confirms Casualties of Anti-Government Riots." *New York Times*, August 2, 1978.

Reuters. "Shah Stresses Commitment to Political Freedom." *New York Times*, August 6, 1978.

"Shah Hanging by a Thread." Editorial. *San Francisco Chronicle*, December 12, 1978.

"The Shah's Divided Land." *Time*, September 18, 1978.

Shelley, Percy. "Ozymandias." In *Poems That Live Forever*, edited by Hazel Felleman, 436. New York, NY: Doubleday, 1965.

"Strikes for More Pay Spread." *Kayhan International* (Tehran, Iran), October 7, 1978.

"Strong 'quakes Rocks Kavir." *Kayhan International* (Tehran, Iran), September 17, 1978.

"Student Defiance in Tehran." *Kayhan International* (Tehran, Iran), October 29, 1978.

"Students, Troops in Clash at University." *Kayhan International* (Tehran, Iran), November 4, 1978.

"Tabriz in Flames."*Tehran Journal*, January 9, 1979.

"Tehran Clashes Leave Trail of Destruction." *Kayhan International* (Tehran, Iran), October 30, 1978.

"Three Killed as Rival Protesters Clash." *Kayhan International* (Tehran, Iran), October 31, 1978.

"Three 'Premiers' in a Day!" *Kayhan International* (Tehran, Iran), October 11, 1978.

Times Wire Services. "Iran Journalists Strike, 3 Anti-Shah Protesters Killed." *Los Angeles Times*, October 12, 1978.

"To All Employees." Called to Hadley Road. In *ABII Bulletin*, Tehran, Iran, December 2, 1978.

"Troops Break Up Tehran Rallies." *Kayhan International* (Tehran, Iran), October 28, 1978.

"Two-Month Tale of Destruction." *Kayhan International* (Tehran, Iran), January 7, 1978.

United Press. "Huge Iran Mob Tries to Sack U.S. Embassy." *San Francisco Chronicle*, December 25, 1978.

United Press. "Iran Battles a Mob—Bloodiest Clash Yet." *San Francisco Chronicle*, December 2, 1978.

United Press. "Iran Troops Fire on Protesters—Warning of Oil Field Sabotage." *San Francisco Chronicle*, November 23, 1978.

United Press. "U.S. Families Advised to Leave Iran." *San Francisco Chronicle*, January 1, 1979.

United Press. "Violent Protests in Tehran, Provinces." *San Francisco Chronicle*, December 26, 1978.

United Press. "Wildcat Power Strike in Tehran." *San Francisco Chronicle*, November 22, 1978.

United Press & Associated Press. "Hundreds Reported Slain by Iran Army." *San Francisco Chronicle*, January 1, 1979.

United Press & Associated Press. "More Yanks Flee Violence in Iran." *San Francisco Chronicle*, January 3, 1979.

United Press & Associated Press. "New Iran Leader Fears Army Coup." *San Francisco Chronicle*, January 11, 1979.

United Press & Associated Press. "New Protests in Iran—6 Cadets Die." *San Francisco Chronicle*, January 15, 1979.

United Press International. "2 Million Marchers Defy Shah." *Press Democrat* (Santa Rosa, CA), December 11, 1978.

United Press International. "65 Safe in Iran Airliner Crash." *New York Times*, July 28, 1978.

United Press International. "Americans Told, 'Stay out of Sight.'" *Press Democrat* (Santa Rosa, CA), December 5, 1978.

United Press International. "Americans Try to Flee Iran: Gunfire in Streets." *Press Democrat* (Santa Rosa, CA), January 2, 1979.

United Press International. "Demonstrators Try to Storm U.S. Embassy." *Press Democrat* (Santa Rosa, CA), December 3, 1978.

United Press International. "Iran Army Using Restraint-U.S." *Kayhan International* (Tehran, Iran), September 11, 1978.

United Press International. "Iranian Army Seizes Town Hit by Riots." *Press Democrat* (Santa Rosa, CA), August 11, 1978. *Ancestry.*

United Press International. "Iran Reports Outbreak of Cholera in Desert Town and at Gulf Port." *New York Times*, July 30, 1978.

United Press International. "Iran Troops Kill Five in Rioting." *Press Democrat* (Santa Rosa, CA), November 5, 1978.

United Press International. "Iran Violence Continues as Civilian Government OK'd." *Press Democrat* (Santa Rosa, CA), January 3, 1979.

United Press International. "Shah Frees 1,200 Prisoners." *Press Democrat* (Santa Rosa, CA), October 25, 1978.

United Press International. "Shah 'Open' to New Government." *Press Democrat* (Santa Rosa, CA), December 19, 1978.

United Press International. "Shah Soon to Leave Iran." *Press Democrat* (Santa Rosa, CA), December 31, 1978.

United Press International. "Shah Wins Battle of Streets." *Press Democrat* (Santa Rosa, CA), November 13, 1978.

United Press International. "Ten Arrested in Fire Attack on Iran Theater." *Press Democrat* (Santa Rosa, CA), August 21, 1978.

United Press International. "Toll Mounts in Iran Riots." *Press Democrat* (Santa Rosa, CA), October 9, 1978.

United Press International. "Violence Halts Iran Exports." *Press Democrat* (Santa Rosa, CA), December 27, 1978.

United Press International. "Weeping Shah Heads for Exile in U.S." *Press Democrat* (Santa Rosa, CA), January 16, 1979.

"U.S. 'Advises Shah to Leave the Country.'" *Kayhan International* (Tehran, Iran), January 10, 1979.

"Violent Protests Continue." *Tehran Journal*, January 9, 1979.

Wallace, Jerry. "Security Update." In *ABII Bulletin*, Tehran, Iran: ABII, October 28, 1978.

Wallace, Jerry. "Security Update." In *ABII Bulletin*, Tehran, Iran: ABII, October 29, 1978.

Wallace, Jerry. "Security Update." In *ABII Bulletin*, Tehran, Iran: ABII, November 4, 1978.

Wallace, Jerry. "Security Update." In *ABII Bulletin*, Tehran, Iran: ABII, November 14, 1978.

Wallace, Jerry. "Security Update." In *ABII Bulletin*, Tehran, Iran: ABII, November 21, 1978.

Wallace, Jerry. "Security Update." In *ABII Bulletin*, Tehran, Iran: ABII, November 28, 1978.

Wallace, Jerry. "Security Update." In *ABII Bulletin*, Tehran, Iran: ABII, December 5, 1978.

Wallace, Jerry. "Security Update." In *ABII Bulletin*, Tehran, Iran: ABII, December 20, 1978.

Wallace, Jerry. "Security Update." In *ABII Bulletin*, Tehran, Iran: ABII, December 23, 1978.

Washington Post. "The March on Tehran: Biggest Anti-Shah Protest Yet." *San Francisco Chronicle*, December 11, 1978.

"Wave of Strikes, Protests Spread." *Kayhan International* (Tehran, Iran), October 9, 1978.

"Well Done Says Khomeini." *Kayhan International* (Tehran, Iran), January 7, 1979.

"Wild Scenes at Mass Funeral." *Kayhan International* (Tehran, Iran), August 23, 1978.

AUTHOR BIO

 John Doolittle lives in Northern California with his wife, Nora. He has a degree in economics and a master's in finance. John retired as a senior executive from Pacific Bell/SBC. He also served in the United States Air Force Reserves, and was a member of the National Ski Patrol. John and Nora both graduated from Occidental College in Los Angeles, California. They have traveled to over forty-five countries, play bridge, golf, and ski. They have two married children with families of their own; one located in Florida and the other in California.